OUR FAITH

BASIC CHRISTIAN BELIEF

Our Faith

Basic Christian Belief

Max Thurian
Brother of Taizé

Translated by Emily Chisholm

CROSSROAD · NEW YORK

136404

1982

The Crossroad Publishing Company
575 Lexington Avenue, New York, N.Y. 10022

© Les Presses de Taizé, France, 1978

Printed in the United States of America

Library of Congress Cataloging in Publication Data

Thurian, Max.
    Our faith, basic Christian belief.

    1. Theology, Doctrinal—Popular works.
2. Christian life—Reformed authors.   I. Title.
BT77.T53   1982   230   82-72008
ISBN 0-8245-0547-6

Translator's Note

The subject of this book can be expressed in a single word — Love. God is love ; that is the mystery of the three Persons in Unity ; God is love in his dealing with humankind, in creation, salvation and sanctification by the means of grace ; Christian life in the Spirit of God is called to be a life overflowing with love, the love we give is the pledge of the Love we receive. The first generation of Christians found it necessary to employ a particular word for the love they had found in Christ — agape. St Jerome employs caritas *in translating the Vulgate and this becomes "charity" in the traditional English versions of the New Testament, (1 Corinthians 13 being the best-known text in which "charity" is employed). Today, "charity" has lost this original sense, (cf. "cold as charity", "charitable institutions"), while the word "love" can mean almost anything. So in these pages, "charity" and "love" are both employed, as equally valid translations of* agape, *in the hope that this will serve to remind readers of all that is meant by these words.*

Emily Chisholm

Contents

INTRODUCTION

The ecumenical dialogue, all the searching for a visible unity between Christians in one single Church, necessarily raises the problem of what the Church believes.

Some people, in their desire to hasten the coming of visible unity, are in danger of underestimating the importance of the content of the Church's faith. They think that as charity is the greatest of all virtues, it should be fairly easy to find agreement on points of controversy. They are inclined to label "conservative" all who believe that unity in truth is vital and that it is something which demands enthusiastic but patient hard work.

Others, who emphasize the demands of the faith, are sometimes in danger of placing obstacles on the road that leads to unity. They feel that truth must be safeguarded at all costs ; better delay unity than compromise doctrinal purity. They are apt to consider that every attempt between Christians to distinguish the essentials of doctrine from their various theological wrappings serves only to confuse the issue.

In both these positions there is a central concern to be obedient to God's will. There can be no question of choosing one aspect of Christian loyalty today, and rejecting the other.

In the search for visible unity there is need for a large degree of doctrinal understanding and an equal degree of ecumenical zeal. We need to have a pastoral concern which seeks to maintain in the truth those entrusted to us, and at the same time seeks to open their minds and hearts to the full dimensions of charity and unity. Only if they are fully aware of the essential truths of the faith can Christians go forward with the sure hope of arriving one day at visible unity in one Church ; but only if they are completely, ecumenically open, eager for charity and unity, will they be able to remain alive and firmly rooted in the faith.

The only firm and lasting foundation for unity will be the truth accepted by common consent, but truth can only be given its full expression where there is charity and a search for unity. So faith is the sure pledge of lasting unity ; and ecumenical openness is the source of a decisive renewal in faith, and deeper knowledge of Christian truth.

The Christian's confrontation with the world around demands this same clear insight into truth and openness in charity. A Christian can be open to the world with sensitive understanding all the more freely if he knows what he believes. At the same time, the Christian can believe all the more deeply and thankfully in so far as he has universal charity, a concern for the truly catholic unity of all mankind in Christ.

In every ecumenical exchange with fellow Christians separated from us by history, as in every fraternal exchange with people who cannot profess faith, we need to be clear if we are to be as open to them as the essence of our Christian faith allows.

We have to love truth, but love of the truth cannot possibly bring us to forget the truth of love. We have to live in charity and seek unity, although the life of charity and the quest of unity cannot possibly bring us to compromise the love of truth in unity. The balance is a delicate one, but trusting prayer enables us to discover a way of discerning, in genuine charity, both loyalty to the truth and the path to unity.

Encounter and dialogue have shown us that our common ground is vaster far than any inherited disagreements. Historical events, psychological differences, misunderstandings based on ignorance, sins caused by the Divider — as well as a loyal but divergent vision of certain obligations of belief — still keep us apart ; but the obstacles that have been discerned are now being removed, while we pray that any which are insurmountable may be broken down by the power of the Resurrection.

Our intention in this book is to express our common Christian Creed, only noting here and there points on which differences remain ; these notes are grouped for convenience at the end of the book. It is good to confess our common faith together to the greatest possible extent, and so show to the world our fundamental unity. It is important that Christians today should know what they believe in common with other Christians, and not only what they disagree about ; in this way charity is kindled from their hearts, by the living presence of Him who both speaks and is the Truth, our Lord Jesus Christ.

Each chapter takes a point of Christian faith and expounds it simply. Readers must not look in such a work for a developed theology, or a detailed exposition of every controversy. Our intention is to help Christians caught up in the rhythms of the modern world, who have no time to read long theological works but want to educate their faith. Of course, problems arise at every step, but we have tried to expound basic Christian truth without always discussing them. Our main concern is the visible unity of Christians in the one Church of Christ.

The forty chapters are divided into three major parts : the Truth, the Way and the Life, following the words of Christ, "I am the Way, the Truth and the Life." Any such division is bound to be artificial, and it is important not to forget that in Christian life everything is truth, everything is way, everything is life. The three terms overlap constantly. In the first part, the Truth, we have tried to bring together elements of basic belief concerning God, the Father, the Son, the Holy Spirit, and concerning the Church — the pattern familiar from the Apostles' Creed. In the second part, the Way, we have grouped chapters about the means of Grace — the ways in which God approaches us, Word and Sacraments, and the ways in which we approach God, personal and liturgical prayer. In the third part, the Life, we have tried to indicate vital points which have an influence on the ways we live day by day, the fruits of charity.

The Truth

1

HOW CAN I BELIEVE?

"Faith means being sure of what we hope for, convinced that realities we cannot see, exist." This simple definition is amply sufficient to understand what faith is [1].

Faith is a sheer gift of God's goodness. In the mystery of his grace, God grants, in his own time, to everyone who encounters Christ, the gift of faith by which to receive the truth.

So faith is the mysterious fruit of a direct action of the Holy Spirit creating in the human heart the necessary spiritual conditions for the union and communion of our whole being with God, for complete confidence in him, for an inward understanding of his Word and for an obedience consecrated to his will.

Faith is first and foremost the gift of communion with God given to man by the Holy Spirit. The Holy Spirit establishes between the human heart he has prepared and Christ whose Word he interprets, a communion of love which is the beginning and end of the whole relationship of faith between God and man.

16

In communion with God to whom he gives himself with his whole heart, man possesses the full
assurance of faith. He enters upon a way that is both
certainty and struggle. He will have the inner light
of the Holy Spirit assuring him completely of the
presence of Christ and the Love of the Father, but he
will often be attacked by the powers of evil, by doubt,
distress and pride, trying to make him lose his faith.
But, in this very struggle faith grows and becomes a
stronger assurance of what we hope for.

The union and communion of man with God
occur in complete confidence in him, an inner understanding of his Word and an obedience consecrated
to his will. There is interplay between the mind and
the will of man, and the realities of salvation accomplished by God for man. Faith has confidence in the
truth which has been revealed, faith understands the
Word of God, faith obeys his will. The man of faith
may experience trials of doubt, the rebellion of his
reason, and even disobedience to God's will. But
through this spiritual combat faith grows stronger
and becomes a more evident proof of the unseen
realities.

Apart from the trials of sin, faith also experiences periods of dryness and darkness, faith is not
always joyous assurance and conspicuous proof.
Faith is not sight. Faith also demands an act of will,
whose source and whose strength are in God, to
overcome those times of dryness and darkness. There
are dark nights of faith when we must be content to
advance with a dim light. At such times faith seems
to be a leap in the dark when we force our wretched-
ness to plunge into the river of the grace of God.
It is perhaps in these times of dryness and darkness
that our faith, weak as it is, appears at its purest ;
without any human support from reason or from
the senses, it is a pure act of trust in God who at the
end of the night will bring the rising of the morning
star.

Faith is not a purely individual act ; bearing and sustaining our personal faith there is the faith of the Church. The realisation that one is not alone in believing, but that a community of people, locally and throughout the world, is present, surrounding the Christian and carrying him in his spiritual combat, is one of the mainstays of faith. God has not called us each on our own, independently of the others ; if he gives his Spirit to each Christian to arouse and to nourish faith within him, he has given the Spirit first and foremost to the Church, the body of Christ, of which each Christian is a member in solidarity with the others.

It is all together then that Christians live their faith, the assurance of faith is a common certitude ; the proof of faith is for all in common. When times of dryness and darkness come, we must rest on the faith of other Christians who believe with us, who in these periods of struggle, believe better and more (perhaps) than we do. And this common faith of the Church, the fruit of the Holy Spirit in her, allows the Christian who is passing through a time of darkness and dryness to return gradually to life again through the inspiration of the faith of the others. At these times we can say to God this ancient prayer from the liturgy : "Regard not our sins but the faith of thy Church"... And the Father who sees us all together in one and the same Christian family, allows the faith of the stronger members to pass into those who are undergoing trials. The faith of the Church gradually becomes once more the faith of each one — even the weakest, the most anxious and the most distressed.

2

WHO GIVES US FAITH?

Grace is God's attitude towards men, an attitude full of love as he watches over them in his providence, pardons them in his mercy and sanctifies them in his goodness. So Grace then, is also the work of God within man, leading him to possession of eternal life for always. Grace is the work of the Holy Spirit in man, transmitting to him the love of the Father and the Son and so enabling him to live in communion with God.

The grace of God is revealed firstly by an act of *election*. God, in his love, choses each man to make him his son and lead him into perfect communion with him. This act of election is completed in acts of *predestination*. God chooses favourable times in every individual's life-history and arranges occasions which will allow him to meet Christ. He anticipates a man's intentions in order to prompt him to choose the path which will lead him to Christ and to the decision to believe in him, to follow and to obey him. Predestination, like election, is an entirely free gift. God does not wait for man's willingness in order to attract him to himself. He goes the whole distance separating him from the heart of sinful man. He comes to plant in it intentions inspired by his grace. It is through sheer generosity on God's part that man can begin to glimpse the light of Christ. The predestination of grace means that behind and before all our positive intentions regarding God, there is an act of the Holy Spirit, guiding our minds and our wills into submission to the love of Christ.

There is an image which can give us an inkling of the mystery of election and predestination. The grace of God can be compared with the power of a river which bears away everything it encounters. Sooner or later men are caught up in this stream of grace which bears them onwards into eternal life. As they are borne along in this great stream, they know that they have contributed nothing to this compelling force which preceded them, tore them from indifference or unbelief and impels them towards the Kingdom of God. They cannot find the source of this grace within themselves ; it is in the first place an external force present before their willingness to receive it ; it is God, who through election and predestination is the source of this grace which urges man on and carries him away in its powerful current. Man, borne onwards by this current of grace preceding him and bearing him up, consents to be carried along by God, and God alone, and that is his salvation. But, as God wants him free, man has the possibility of resisting the stream, he can cling to the river bank. In this case he refuses to allow himself to be borne onwards by God, he resists the flow of grace and so prepares his downfall. Salvation is consent to the grace whose power compels us on every side ; the sin against the Spirit which could lead to our downfall is stubborn resistance to grace.

Chosen and predestined in this way, man, borne along by the river of grace, hears the call of

God, his *vocation* to the Christian life. Calling man to believe in him, to trust and to obey him, God gives him also strength to accept this vocation. The yes which he speaks in his heart, is said by man himself, but it is thanks to the Holy Spirit who reveals to him the joy of consenting. Without the grace of the Holy Spirit's presence, man could not welcome the call of God, but, in spite of this presence, he could resist the vocation God addresses to him. The consent of his whole being to the grace of God is therefore necessary, a human consent for which he receives the strength of the Holy Spirit who comes to convince his heart.

The positive response of man to the calling of God, re-establishes him in the *communion* of a son with the Father, that communion lost through sin. This communion with God restores to man all the possibilities of recovering the values of his original nature. He lives this communion by faith, which is the gift of his whole being to the love of the Father, a faithful attachment to Christ and genuine availability to the Holy Spirit.

In this communion with God by faith man is justified and sanctified. *Justification* by faith, which takes place in the restored communion with the Father, in life in Christ and by the Holy Spirit, is the gift of mercy God offers to man : he forgives all his sin, he justifies him, he makes him good in his sight because man has put his whole trust in him. God does not justify man on account of his moral and spiritual virtues, all he asks of him is faith and his total attachment, in order to pronounce him good and to forgive everything.

This justification however, continues in *sanctification*. When God justifies a man by giving him the grace of restored communion with him by faith, he also sanctifies him so that faith may bear all its fruits. Man, justified and forgiven by reason of the faith which unites him to God, must consent to the transformation of his life which the Holy Spirit desires to effect. The sanctification of the Christian's life, willed by the Father who has justified him because of his faith, develops in union with Christ who died and rose for us, and by the Holy Spirit who works in us by the word of God and the sacraments of his presence. But, if it is the Holy Spirit who effects our sanctification and causes our faith to bear all the fruits of charity, we must continually give our consent to this act of the Spirit by which our whole being is transfigured. Sin, continually springing up again within us, can compromise this sanctification ; we have to allow it to be conquered by the weapons of the Holy Spirit who is fighting in us and for us until we reach the goal of our life's race and enter into God's Kingdom.

3

WHERE CAN I FIND THE FAITH?

The place where Christian truth can be found is a collection of books and written texts, the Holy Scriptures, because Christian truth is an historical truth ; now, historical truth is attested by documents which state the facts and the interpretation of those facts.

The Christian faith is not a religion founded on myths, poetic but non-historic explanations of the mysteries concerning divinity and humanity. It is not based upon rites, rituals of initiation which lead to knowledge of these mysteries. It is not based upon a philosophy, a body of metaphysical ideas explaining the mysteries of God and the destiny of man. It is not based on a mysticism, a scheme of contemplative asceticism which gradually brings man under the influence of the divinity.

Certainly, because of its humanity, because the word of God is expressed in human language, there are in the Christian faith, myths, rites, philosophy and mysticism ; but these are secondary elements, religious instruments which do not fully express the essential meaning of the Christian faith : essentially and basically it is a relationship between man and God, initiated by God alone — God who spoke and still speaks to man, God who lived and still lives with man ; it is based, then, on a history, the sacred history of the relationship between God and man, attested by written documents, the Holy Scriptures.

But the Christian faith is not only a religion of the Holy Book, even although the Bible does contain the complete revelation of God in history [2]. Christian faith is a life in community gathered around the Word of God. We shall return later to this communal aspect of the Christian faith. We begin now with Holy Scriptures which bear the Word of God, spoken in history for the happiness of mankind.

The Holy Scriptures consist of an initial collection of books revealing the Word of God proclaimed before the coming of Christ : the Old Testament. These texts which report the history of the people of Israel, a people chosen by God to proclaim his Word, were read by Christ during his earthly life. He read them as containing the very Word of God, enshrining the progressive revelation of God to men, the medium gradually revealing the truth, to men isolated from God by sin. So these ancient texts come to us with the guarantee of Christ's divine authority which assures us that they are divine revelation. The

Christian reads the Old Testament and prays the psalms, following the example of Christ and is certain, as he was, that the truth about God and man is found in their pages, clothed in the stories of the history of one people, the people of God, Israel.

Certainly all the texts of the Old Tesament do no belong to the same literary category. There are historical books, which are documents on the facts of Israel's history with a religious interpretation of those facts. There are poetic texts which sing the glory of God and the hopes of man. There are religious myths belonging to the common treasury of all, explaining the great mysteries of creation, sin and the origins of the world. But all these texts, history, poetry or myth are a language used by God to speak to men.

Even though the inspired writers drew on the treasuries of religion, myth and poetry of mankind to explain for instance, the mystery of the origin of this world (the Book of Genesis), the Word of God spoke through their literary compositions so that the essential truth about creation, sin and the grace of God might be revealed. So, those texts whose themes can be found in other religions have an aim and a finality very different from theirs because they contain the revelation of God as Creator. Their proclamation declares the truth about the origins of the world. We must not halt at their literary, mythical or poetic form, believing we can find there detailed facts of an event in history; we must penetrate their profound intention, the very Word of God which made use of these human, religious myths as a language for communicating the truth about the first beginning.

The second collection of texts of Holy Scripture, the New Testament, is essentially a collection of historical testimony to the event of the incarnation of God in Jesus Christ to liberate the human race.

The apostles chosen by Christ, eye-witnesses of his life, death and resurrection, attentive hearers of his teaching, and their direct successors, wrote gospels and epistles. They, as pillars of the Church, had received from Christ the promise of the gift of the Spirit, who would bring back to their memories the words and the gestures of their Master. The New Testament writers were inspired by the Holy Spirit in recounting the events of Christ's life and in interpreting them. « The Holy Spirit whom the Father will send in my name, will teach you everything and remind you of what I told you... He will lead you into the whole truth » (John 14, 26 ; 16, 13). The Church has always believed that the writers of the New Testament were inspired in this way ; in any case she did not fix the list of these inspired writings from the start. She waited for their authority to impose itself upon her before deciding definitely on their number.

The Early Church recognised, by an infallible decision, in the New Testament as we have it today, the collection of inspired books that was to form the source of her knowledge of Christ and her rule of faith. By this she did not mean that the Word of God could not overflow these limits ; but, in her humble service of truth she was excluding any other text on Christ or the Early Church from possessing the absolute authority of the very Word of God. The truth had imposed itself on the Church, as Christ had imposed himself on the apostles, and, inspired by the Holy Spirit, gave a standard of her thinking so that she would remain faithful to Christ.

Urged on by the Holy Spirit to recognise in the Scriptures the Word of God as decisive for her faith, the Church has always believed in the inspiration of the writings of the New Testament. The experience of her preaching, always renewed, always inexhaustible, on these inexhaustible texts has only confirmed her conviction of the inspiration of the Scriptures.

First comes the question of the inspiration of the writers of the New Testament, the apostles or the apostles' successors. They inherited the promise of Christ, quoted above, and received the Holy Spirit who recalled the facts and the words of Christ to their memories, or guided them in the choice of their source ; they received the Holy Spirit who led them into the whole truth, as they interpreted these facts and these words of Christ, or when they were deducing from the first teaching of Christian theology and Christian ethics.

So it is not only a question of the inspiration of individuals but also of the inspiration of their act of writing, so that we can speak of the divine inspiration of the text of the Scriptures, as well as of the apostles and their successors who wrote the New Testament.

Such inspiration of the authors and of the sacred writings does not exclude the human characteristics of these individuals and of these texts. The inspiration of the authors and of their writings does not imply the inspiration of every word of these writings. There is no literal inspiration, as if the Holy Spirit had simply dictated to the authors of Holy Writ. The Holy Spirit, acting on the memory, judgment and reason of these authors, inspired them to write a text whose content is the Word of God and whose literary form proceeds from their own humanity. The divine inspiration of the content which is God's Word does not imply inspiration, for each individual word, for the literary categories, syntax and grammar ; nor does it imply the absolute accuracy of the chronology or the details of a narrative. In fact one of the proofs of the historicity of a narrative is that it is set out in a different form and with differing details in the various accounts offered by the four evangelists. As the event had made a different impact on the mind of each witness, their narratives were different, even although the Holy Spirit inspired each of them in the act of writing his account.

An analogy can be drawn between the mystery of Christ and the mystery of Scripture. Jesus Christ has two natures, being true God and true man, in the unity of the person of the Son of God incarnate. Scripture, by analogy (for the mystery of Christ is unique), has also two natures, it is a truly human document as to outward form, a truly inspired text as to content — the Word of God making unity of the human form and the inspired content. Just as we must never deny nor neglect the humanity of Christ in order to know the incarnate Son of God in his divinity, so we must never deny nor neglect the human form of Scriptures in order to discern the Word of God. It is in Christ's humanity that we encounter his divinity as the incarnate Son of God ; it is in the human form of the Scriptures that we discover their divine content : the Word of God, present in the inspired text when it is read and preached.

The New Testament comprises :

— historical words and facts ;
— apostolic interpretations of these words and facts ;
— theological dissertations on these words and these facts.

The historical facts and words of the life of Christ have been reported for us in accounts which have to be received in faith but on which historical and literary criticism can be exercised. The aim of such criticism is to help us discern the human form of the apostolic witness, so enabling us to penetrate more deeply into the inspired content of their testimony which is the very Word of God.

The facts and the historical words of Christ's life had an interpretation put upon them by the apostles or their successors. Led by the Holy Spirit into the whole truth, they were able to give the first authentic interpretation of what they had seen and heard. This apostolic interpretation is inspired as is the account of the facts and the words of the life of Christ. It is to be found in the Epistles, but equally in the Gospels which provide us with the facts and the historical words, together with a preliminary interpretation of them by the gospel-writers. Here criticism can help us to disentangle the facts and the words from the immediate interpretation put upon them by the gospel-writers, or by the sources they used. But this work must not lead us to neglect the apostolic interpretation in favour of so-called pure historical truth. Besides the fact that criticism often remains susceptible of further verification, apostolic interpretation is inspired, as is the historical account of the facts and the words to which it refers. The Word of God is present in the apostolic interpretation as well as in the historical account.

Lastly, the historical words and facts of the life of Christ are the subject matter of theological dissertations dictated to the gospel-writers either by the experience of life in the apostolic Church, or by a desire to draw a parallel between the Old Covenant and the New, or by some other consideration. The accounts in St. John's Gospel, while reporting the historical words and facts, have been shown to be arranged according to a plan, illustrating the sacramental life of the Early Church, as she celebrated baptism and the Eucharist. The first two chapters of St. Luke's Gospel have been shown to relate the incarnation and the childhood of Christ, in terms of images and texts from the Old Testament... If the facts and the historical words of Christ's life are respected in such theological compositions, perhaps their chronological order is not, for the author is more concerned to pursue a general scheme of teaching than to preserve a chronological order and details he considered accessory. The words of Christ may also be the object of development echoing primitive apostolic preaching especially in St. John. But here too the theological writing is inspired and transmits the Word of God ; it cannot be neglected on pretext of retaining only authentic facts and words.

Historical facts and words, interpretations by the apostles and theological writings about these words and facts, interweave to form the inspired text of the Scriptures. Throughout the entire text in which criticism may discern the various super-imposed strata (but should never treat one layer in isolation) the Word of God reverberates, and makes an indissoluble unity of the human and inspired elements.

So it is that Holy Scripture is the place to find the truth. It is the unfailing channel that from Christ, the Word of God incarnate, Source of Revelation, transmits to the Church and the Christian, enlightened by the Holy Spirit, the truth in its original fullness.

4

WHERE TO LIVE THE FAITH?

Christian faith is not the religion of a book but a life of prayer, hope and charity lived in community around the Lord whose Word is heard in Holy Scripture. So, the truth which comes to us from Scripture, is received by the community of the Church, in the milieu prepared by the Holy Spirit in which this truth can be understood, proclaimed and believed most authentically.

Christ, who founded the Church, the universal community of all who are baptised, continues to build her up, teach her and nourish her by his Word contained in Scripture, and by the Holy Spirit. The Church is being continually revitalised by the living Word of God and by the Holy Spirit in that event which is the proclamation of the truth contained in Holy Scripture.

The Church receives the Word of God which ceaselessly refashions her continuity ; she receives the Word of God contained in Holy Scripture as she proclaims it in her liturgy and in her preaching, in her study and her teaching of it. Since the Word of God is addressed first and foremost to the people of God, the Church, and since the Holy Spirit is given first of all to the Church, as a universal body, it is the Church which is the privileged environment where the truth can be heard and understood [3].

The Church is « the household of God, the pillar and the buttress of the truth » (1 Tim. 3. 15), the universal community inspired by the Holy Spirit which can receive and proclaim most truthfully the Word of God contained in Scripture. Of course the Holy Spirit teaches the truth to each member of the Church individually as he listens to the Word of God from Scripture, but no individual judgment can lay claim to the truth, unless it is in accord with the universal judgment of the Church. The universal judgment of the Church is the norm of right interpretation of the Word of God, since the Holy Spirit gives to the universal Church the true sense of Holy Scripture by enlightening her with the Word of God itself. In this way, the Holy Spirit and the Word of God direct the Church and assist her in proclaiming the truth.

This direction and assistance of the Church by the Holy Spirit and the Word of God were first manifested in the apostles. Christ began to build his Church on the foundation of the apostles and the prophets, on the foundation of the eye-witnesses of his life, death and resurrection (the apostles), or on that of their immediate successors (the prophets of the New Covenant). These apostles and prophets received inspiration to proclaim the Word of God and to write down the text containing it. They also had the responsibility of government and teaching with the help of the Holy Spirit and the Word of God.

On one hand, the office of the apostolate is unique and intransmissible in character : only the apostles and their immediate successors received inspiration to transmit the Word of God and were the foundations of the Church. Therefore their ministry is still living and relevant. The apostles and the prophets continue to direct the Church by the initial interpretation of the Word of God which they gave : they also assist the Church by their prayers and teaching with the help of the Holy Spirit and the Word of God.

But, on the other hand, the office of the apostolate, established by Christ, has a permanent character which is transmissible : the ministers of the Church who have the responsibility of government and the custody of doctrine, share in the office of the apostolate. So, throughout her history the universal community of the Church has been directed and instructed so as to remain obedient to the Word of God and in the unity of the Holy Spirit.

If there are ministers of the Church who have the special duty of governing the Church and of watching over her teaching, this does not imply that the body of the faithful remains passive, simply allowing themselves to be led and taught. The environment in which the truth is understood and proclaimed is the body of the Church of Christ in its entirety. Every Christian who reads the Scriptures and bears witness, shares effectively in the universal understanding of the Word of God. There are, of course, theologians who are called more specifically to search deeply into the Scriptures in order to bring out all the aspects of the truth ; there are of course, pastors called more specifically to keep doctrine consonant with the truth ; but every Christian united with the world-wide community of the Church, enlightened by his instructors and guided by his pastors, plays his part in the deepening of doctrinal knowledge and in the preservation of the deposit of truth.

At certain points in her history when she is threatened by false doctrine or when she needs to bring her proclamation of the truth up to date once more, the Church meets in ecumenical council. Here the entire global community is represented by its leaders and seeks new formulation of the one and only truth. The decisions of an ecumenical council bind the whole community of the universal Church, which is obliged to accept as the truth the conciliar expression of the Word of God. An ecumenical council is the privileged moment in the life of the Church when the universal understanding of truth is clarified under the guidance of the Holy Spirit.

Knowledge of the truth, given in its fullness in the Scriptures, is thus deepened in the course of the centuries within the communion of the Church, each individual bringing his contribution of thought and prayer to deepening knowledge of the Word of God in the light of the Holy Spirit. To have a true understanding of the Word of God contained in Scripture, it is good to adhere to the ecumenical sense of truth held by the universal Church, in which the Holy Spirit resides.

5

DOES THE FAITH CHANGE?

The Word of God, contained in Holy Scripture, read and proclaimed in the Church, finds expression in the life of the Church in the form of tradition. Tradition is :

— the life of the Word of God in the Church ;
— the act by which the Church transmits the Word;
— the result of this life and act.

The words and deeds of Christ were at first transmitted by oral tradition. Gradually written texts appeared which were collected to form the New Testament ; but these written texts did not put a stop to the tradition which had produced them ; the tradition continued to provide a living commentary on these inspired documents. Certainly, because of their stable nature, the inspired texts became normative for the life of the Church and its living tradition. It was perfectly natural for the Church to refer to the inspired writings to justify her living tradition. But tradition reflected in a living way within the Church what the inspired writers had recorded of the Word of God in their texts. Tradition transmitted the spirit of the apostolic family for the authentic interpretation of the Word of God contained in the inspired normative texts ; this « family spirit » is the Holy Spirit received by the Church as she interprets the Word of God.

To take an example — the Lord's Supper, celebrated by Christ on the evening of Holy Thursday, was repeated by the apostles, and this practice, together with the accompanying words, was transmitted live by the primitive apostolic tradition. Then texts by Matthew, Mark, Luke and Paul appeared, reporting the essential actions and words of Christ. These inspired texts are normative for the authentic celebration and understanding of the Eucharist. A scientific study of the texts, words and ritual of the paschal meal from which Jesus drew his inspiration, can lead to deeper understanding of what Christ intended to do and what the Church must do after him. The primitive Church however did not restrict herself to the sacred writings for her celebration of the Eucharist. She lived the sacrament in a framework of prayers, songs, gestures and attitudes about which the inspired texts tell us nothing ; she had a eucharistic tradition which gave to these texts their living context in the practice of the Church. This tradition evolved and grew richer until it produced in the 4th and 5th centuries the great liturgical families in which we still live the Eucharist today. If we tried to reduce the celebration of the Lord's Supper to the bare texts of the New Testament, we would be left with a very impoverished liturgy, cut off from the family spirit of the Church, which has never ceased to live the celebration of the Eucharist in the tradition which goes back to the apostles. True, there have been unfortunate additions and distortions made at times when the Church no longer possessed a truly liturgical spirit ; but it is precisely in such cases that the sacred texts, properly studied can play their part as normative authorities, just as the return to the ancient liturgical and patristic sources can lead us to rediscover a tradition, a real life of Eucharist in the Church. The Church today enters into the significance of the Lord's Supper, certainly by studying those New Testament texts reporting Christ's gestures and words, but also by celebrating the Eucharist in accordance with the great liturgical tradition that communicates to her the spirit of the Christian family, the living understanding of the mystery, brought by the Holy Spirit who is alive within her.

Tradition is therefore the life and the transmission of the Word of God in the Church; it is not unimportant to know how the Holy Spirit has led the Church through the centuries in obedience to the Word of God. That can help the Church to avoid many useless detours and many exhausting fresh starts.

This life and transmission of the Word of God in the Church leaves its signs. We have seen this in the liturgical tradition of the Eucharist, but there are also dogmatic signs formed by the credal statements in the creeds and the decisions of the ecumenical councils. Although they do not possess the absolute authority of the inspired Scriptures, the creeds and the conciliar texts have a normative authority, for they express how the universal Church, assisted by the Holy Spirit has understood the Word of God and handed it on to future generations.

The two great creeds expressing the faith, the Apostles' Creed and the Nicene - Constantinople creed, together with the trinitarian and christological definitions, formulated at Nicaea (in 325), at Constantinople (in 381), at Ephesus (in 431) and at Chalcedon (in 451), are recognised as normative by all the major Christian Churches. Certainly, a new ecumenical council could reconsider any given affirmation, in order to complete it or explore it further (which distinguishes a traditional text from an unalterable scriptural text), but until this new council the whole Church is bound to maintain faithfully the conciliar tradition which expresses the Word of God in the life of the Church [4].

We have seen that Scripture, the revelation of the Word of God to the Church, and tradition, the life and transmission of that Word in the Church, were closely linked. We must now explain how Scripture is understood by and in the Church for faithful transmission of the apostolic deposit. The Church's understanding of Scripture is universal, prayerful and missionary.

The Church is universal both in space and in time. In her tradition the Church therefore seeks to explain the Word of God in such a way as to include the understanding of all the local Churches across the world. This is the reason for gathering the Church in ecumenical councils. In her tradition the Church also seeks to explain the Word of God in continuity with past generations of Christians. This is why she returns to liturgical and patristic sources and studies the development of her theology throughout the centuries.

The Church comes to an understanding of the Word of God in her liturgy and transmits it by her liturgical tradition. This is the prayerful aspect of the understanding and tradition of the Word of God by the Church. Holy Scripture furnishes a great part of the Church's language in her liturgy. God speaks to her in the Scriptures ; and, using the words of scripture in psalms and in prayers interwoven with biblical vocabulary, she makes response to God in praise and supplication. In the celebration of the sacraments she actually lives by the Word of God on which she feeds. By this lavish use of scripture in her liturgy, the Church to some extent experiences in a living way the Word of God and this experience is one essential form of tradition. The Church never better understands the truth revealed in Scripture than when she comes to prayer, to worship God and intercede on behalf of all mankind. The liturgy then, is a special place where the Church encounters truth and lives by it ; the liturgy is an essential form of the faithful tradition of the Word of God.

Finally, the Church understands the Word of God and transmits it by being sensitive to the world to which she has to proclaim salvation. This is the missionary form of the Church's understanding and transmission of the Word of God. Christ reigns over the world and mysteriously prepares men to encounter him. The Church must not only know the revelation, but be alert to the signs of this preparation of people's hearts by the Lord of the world. The dialogue of the Church with the world may be one form of tradition. This dialogue widens the Church to her catholic dimensions. For there to be a real tradition of the gospel, for the living Word of God really to penetrate into the present-day life of men and the world, the Church must be profoundly present to men and the world. She must understand them as they are, by living among them. She must above all pierce the values and the vocabulary of the age. By vocabulary we mean all forms of expression, not only language, but the images, the signs, literature, novels, the cinema, the theatre, etc. Every new technique must be considered worthwhile by the Church, with optimism and gratitude. The Church is sometimes pessimistic and puritanical about the world. If it is right for her to reject sin in all its forms, war, injustice, greed and pride, which use the values of this world for their own ends, she must be positive and profoundly hopeful as regards the values themselves, for she can consider them capable of being sanctified by the Gospel. The dialogue of the Church, present to the world and to all its values, with modern man whose language she speaks and understands, then becomes a magnificent occasion when the Gospel finds a new way of expressing itself and so reveals its universality and its effectiveness. The world and all the authentic values which the Lord maintains and develops in it, thus comes to share in a faithful tradition of the Gospel which in every age reveals the wealth of its treasures.

6

WHO IS GOD?

Belief in God is a necessity and a mystery. Without faith in God human existence is absurd. If there is no God, the world, nature and man have no point, for they are only moving towards death and destruction. What significance have the births and lives of countless millions whose only end is death ? Then too, how could nature and man be constituted in such a perfect order if there were no supreme intelligence presiding over the creation of all that is and maintaining it in an ordered existence ? For instance the complicated and subtle perfection of the human body cannot be simply the result of millenial evolution unless a superior mind had guided that evolution to the marvellous fulfilment we now see. Without the existence of God human life is absurd and inexplicable. Without faith in God man arrives at the conviction of the absurdity of his inexplicable life.

But faith in God is a mystery. Any thought of the invisible, universal and eternal existence of God brings us into a tremendous mystery. God can be neither imagined nor conceived ; every represent-ation of God is bound to betray his nature and plunge us into a gulf of insoluble questions. How could we imagine one single being at the origin of all things, the universality of his presence ; — his eternity without beginning ?

Faith in God lies between the necessary rejection of the absurdity of human existence without God and the impossible rational comprehension of the mystery of God's existence, universality and eternity. Faith in God is acceptance of the necessary mystery of God.

Certainly, St. Paul writes to the Romans : "All that we can know of God is plain to see, his invisible nature, namely his eternal power and divinity, has been discerned by the human mind since creation first began"... (Rom. 1. 19-20). But the objective possibility of knowing the existence of God, his eternal power and his divinity, only leads to idolatry and moral disorder, because of human sin. St. Paul describes these aberrations at length.

Faith in God, then, is not natural to man. Contemplating nature he might come to know the essential about God, but sin darkens his mind and leads him astray ; he is only capable of an elementary religion when he ought to be giving glory and thanks to God. However, the possibility of knowing God and offering him spiritual worship makes man conscious of his guilt.

If we consider certain developed religions, which unlike Israel and the Church, have not received an objective revelation of the Word of God, and which nevertheless have developed a certain knowledge of God, a spiritual worship and a contemplative prayer, we have to admit that God in his providence, has influenced those religious groups to keep them from gross idolatry and moral disorder, bringing them towards genuine spirituality and preparing them to receive one day the message of Christ, God and Saviour. If we think of India in particular and its highly developed forms of religion, we cannot but recognise this providential working of God.

In any case, every form of worship, however rudimentary, shows how man aspires to a religion, and to a relationship with God, even if faith in God in the Jewish and Christian sense is not natural to him. He shows that some reminiscence of God persists in his heart and makes him long for a relationship with this unknown God. In his goodness God may direct this aspiration and raise it to spiritual religious sentiment ; this is not a revelation but a help granted by God to every human being, for he has never abandoned anyone — not in any sector of his existence. There is but one God ; so it is to him, and him alone, that all religious worship and all individual prayers ascend. Although they do not know God in all his truth, and in accordance with his revelation, yet all non-Christians who have a religious faith and who search for a relationship between man and God by worship and prayer, address the true God of whose saving acts they know nothing, and God cannot but answer them and lead them on to the knowledge of his grace revealed in Jesus Christ, in Holy Scripture.

For this reason the Church pronounces positively on every spiritual religion as she seeks to discern everywhere signs of God at work and elements of truth which he may have helped men to discover, outside of his revelation.

The Church which is really "catholic", which includes in her communion everyone who is advancing towards the light and already possesses one spark of the light, rejoices in truth wherever she finds it, and recognises the working of the love of

God who desires to enlighten everybody and lead all into truth in all its fullness.

If we possessed only our rational human knowledge of God, if all we knew of him was his existing, his universality, his eternity and his power, our rudimentary faith could not bring us the joy and peace given by the whole truth [5]. Our faith would go no further than to refuse the absurdity of a world without God, accepting intellectually or emotionally an unknown and distant God as the only possible explanation of our human destiny. Such a belief is not yet the Christian faith which gives the peace and the joy of a personal and living encounter with God revealed in Jesus Christ and communicated by the Holy Spirit.

The Christian faith in God is also a refusal to accept the absurdity of atheism : it too is an acceptance of the mystery of God, but it is infinitely more than that. Christian faith in God is personal, living encounter between man and God, in which God has taken the initiative. The specific and unique character of Christian faith in God is that it is addressed to a God who is personal, living, close at hand : the incarnation of God in Jesus Christ makes Christian faith a specific and unique reality compared with other religious faiths.

7

THE TRINITY

Christian belief in God is faith in God-Trinity, Father, Son and Holy Spirit, one God in three equal persons. This Trinity of God is an unfathomable mystery, which can only be approached in the contemplation of faith, founded on the history of salvation as reported for us in Holy Scripture. We do not explain the three persons in the one God, we recognise them in the revelation of the Word of God, as understood by the Church in her tradition ; we adore them in the liturgy of community worship and in personal prayer.

God, creator and saviour, revealed himself in his fullness in Christ. Jesus Christ in his mission on earth revealed to men that God is Father at the origin of all things, creating the world and taking the initiative in salvation. It was the person of the Father in God who sent the Son into the world to manifest his love and to effect universal salvation. The person of the Son, incarnate in a man, manifested, by his life of obedience and his liberating death, the relationship of love which God had established and then restored between himself and men. After the return of Christ to the Father, God sent into his Church the Holy Spirit promised by the Son. The Holy Spirit quickens the Church and grants her all the gifts she needs for her ministry in the world. Since Pentecost the Father and the Son are present in the Church in the person of the Holy Spirit ; all three reign equally over the world to guide it towards the coming eternal Kingdom. God the Father came to us in the Son whom he sent ; the Father and the Son come to us in the Holy Spirit who dwells in the Church and in each Christian ; the Church and the individual Christian come to the Son and the Father by the Holy Spirit.

So Christian faith and prayer are addressed to the Father, through the Son, in the Holy Spirit. It is the Holy Spirit who engenders the faith and prayer which he brings to the Father through the Son. There is perfect equality of the persons of the godhead and complete unity in their action in the Church and in the world. Belief in the Holy Spirit is belief in the Son and the Father ; prayer to the Father is prayer to the Son and the Holy Spirit. This equality does not abolish the distinction between the persons of the godhead. It is the Father who sent the Son by the Holy Spirit, at the incarnation. It is the Father who sent the Holy Spirit in the name of the Son at Pentecost. It is the Son who took flesh in obedience to the Father by the power of the Holy Spirit. It is the Holy Spirit who was given to the Church at Pentecost and dwells in the hearts of Christians to give them faith and prayer, that rises to the Father through the Son.

This faith in God-Trinity, based on the revelation of the history of salvation and the fruit of liturgical and personal contemplation, brings us to the mystery of the life of God, without being able to understand it rationally. There is not solitude in God, but a community of equal persons in perfect unity. Although incomprehensible to reason, this mystery of the Trinity of God is more accessible to our faith than the affirmation of a single divine person. With three persons existing in Trinity, God becomes more accessible to us and closer, for he reveals himself as a living God, into whose life we can enter by faith and prayer. He reveals himself also as a God of love in whom distinct and equal persons love one another in the absolute perfection of love. Faith and prayer are not distant terrifying dialogue of a creature with its creator alone in his divinity, they are the participation of us men, who have become the adopted sons of the Father, through the Son, in the Holy Spirit, in the dialogue and exchange of the three divine persons in perfect love and unity.

8

THE FATHER ALMIGHTY

Within his divine life, God revealed himself as a Father full of love for the Son and the Holy Spirit ; in his divine nature he is already far removed from terrible and distant majesty. It was never God's will to be in solitude ; God is love and this love appears in God's very nature, as fatherly love begetting the Son and from which the Holy Scripture proceeds. In his very nature, God exists to love and to give himself.

Faith in God the Father, as Christ has revealed him to us, straightway sets the believer in a relationship of brotherhood towards the other Christians in the Church, as well as towards all men destined for salvation by God, the universal Father.

As Father, God establishes the whole creation in the unity of a great universal family. God knows none of our limitations and our frontiers. Because he has created all things, he sees the whole creation, in spite of sin, in the unity of its origin and its end. It is man who, through sin, has erected barriers between the creatures.

Then, the Father sees the great human family which he destines for salvation through his Son Jesus Christ. He invites all men to consider themselves brothers in the single family of which he is the Father. He knows each one of his human sons, he hears their stammered prayers and their religious striving after him, he follows them and guides them in their history ; he leads them towards decisive encounter with his Son in the Gospel.

Then within the great human family, the Father sees the Christian family of those baptised, established in the household of God, called to lead their brother men to recognise the Saviour of all.

The contemplation of the Father sets the divisions between Christians in their proper perspective, a sin, unworthy of those who have been wonderfully adopted, all together in one baptism, to form one single body radiating the love of Christ in the midst of the human family.

We have all of us been baptised in the name of the Father, the Son and the Holy Spirit, and so incorporated into that great universal body, which is called the Body of Christ, the Church. This one baptism makes us all brothers in a single family whose Father is God. We all believe the essential truths of the faith of the gospels. Charity binds us together and, as St. Paul says, this charity believes everything, meaning that we must trust each other completely, not being afraid of one another and not opposing one another. Since we have been incorporated in this way into one family, even though there are temporary dissensions within the family, we must today do everything in our power for this family to recover its profound visible unity.

The Father is almighty. His power is at the service of his love. Since he knows and loves every individual in the world, he places at the service of his fatherly love his almighty providence. He directs the events of history, preventing the sin of men from provoking irreparable disasters. He foresees the birth of each individual so as to give him those particular natural graces which will form his unique and irreplaceable personality. He follows him throughout his life, protecting and guiding him so that nothing irreparable happens to prevent him being free to welcome Christ when he encounters him. God decides on his death, in his good time, so that a man has nothing to fear from the dangers of life. In the hand of the Father, man is in perfect safety ; nothing important can happen to him unless God permits it — nor any lesser event — which does not enter into his general destiny, foreseen and in the mind of the Father.

9

THE CREATOR

God, who is living love created the universe so that he could love it and give himself to it. First he created the unseen world, the angelic creatures who represent him and act in his name. These angels live unseen among us, accomplishing the mission God has entrusted to them. The creation and the existence of the angels manifest the personal nature of God who is not a vague spirit diffused over all creation. God is in three persons and uses the angels in his service ; the thinking and acting of God are personal and turn into the thinking and acting of persons serving and obeying him. We are assured that the guardian angels are present beside us, guaranteeing our protection and executing God's providence concerning us.

This angelic-world also has a liturgical function. Joining with the prayers of men, the angels sing the praises of God, the creator and redeemer. They are present in the liturgy of the Church giving her fervour in worship and thanksgiving. They bear before God the prayers of Christians who, in this way are united in the liturgy of heaven. In this worship they join with all the Christians who have died and who are awaiting the establishment in glory of the eternal Kingdom. When Scripture speaks of heaven, it simply means the unseen world whose presence surrounds us : God, the angels and the saints, though invisible, close us round and in a sense live with us. When we speak of heaven, the unseen world, angels and saints, we can only do so in images, for this is a world beyond our limited human conceiving. These images are only approximations, opening our minds to the contemplation of the mystery of God's being, his love and his providence.

God is creator of the earth and of the whole visible world. The first book of the Bible, Genesis, presents this creation of the universe by God alone, as his love moves to supply a subject for its loving. The first chapters of Genesis must not be taken as historical accounts. The sacred writers have used religious myths from many religions as a mould, so to speak, in which to cast the revelation of the Word of God. This mythical form is a kind of poetic language used by the inspired writers to proclaim God's Word on creation : it is God and God alone who is at the origin of all creatures, of the mineral, vegetable and animal kingdoms, and finally of man, the crown of creation.

It is this revelation about creation and also about God's control of the early history of the universe and of man, which is the essential message of Genesis. This revelation does not adopt any particular scientific position. It leaves a clear field for metaphysical conceptions of the origins, so long as the affirmation of the creation and directing of these origins by God is maintained. He conducted the physical and psychical process which resulted in the visible word as we know it, and he will continue to direct it until the final transformation when the new heaven and the new earth appear.

It is possible to think that the creation of the visible world by God consisted in the appearance of the initial physical conditions which, under the direction of God himself, gradually took shape to form, after a sequence of chaos and providential choices, the geological universe as we know it. Then God caused life to appear, vegetable then animal, in an evolution which he continued to direct and in which he made the necessary choices. Finally, at the end of this creative evolution directed by God, man appeared as the beloved and obedient partner of Creation's Master.

The poetic division of the Genesis narrative into six symbolic days is a way of relating God's work, accomplished over long periods of time, with man's work, six days a week with the seventh day for rest. In this poetic description of the creation of the world, Adam and Eve symbolize the first human inhabitants of the earth, that primitive humanity which God had brought into existence, that was not only spiritual, but conscious, personal and responsible.

The focus of the creation narratives on the earth as the heart of the universe, and on primitive man as the crown of creation does not, of course, exclude the possibility that other evolved beings, conscious and intelligent children of God, have been created elsewhere on some other planet in the universe. Christian faith does not have to pronounce on such questions which come within the field of science. Faith does not imply a doctrine of the universe, a cosmology; it only affirms that all things have been created by God who maintains them in existence and quickens them with his energy.

For God, the creator of all things, continues his work of creation, causing all that exists to evolve continuously towards fulfilment. All matter is in his power, and progresses towards fulfilment, directed as it is by the wisdom and the energy of God. On condition that they are placed at man's service and his welfare in God's will, all the discoveries of science, all the achievements of physics and biology gradually bring to light that supreme divine intelligence which controls matter, bringing it to the glory of the new creation from which evil and its power of destruction will be excluded, once and for all.

10

SIN

The first human beings, created by the love of God and for the love of God, were tempted by selfishness and pride and rebelled against God. They wanted to live independently, free from any obedience to the Creator : they wanted to make themselves gods. They rejected the will of God, and his love.

Original sin consists in rebellion against God by man, considering himself the centre of the world and wanting everything to focus on himself ; wanting to dominate others and to live his life for pleasure and nothing else. The story of the fall of Adam and Eve presents this symbolically. Adam and Eve stand for all primitive humanity : the name Adam signifies "he who is drawn out of the earth", and the name Eve "she from whom life is drawn". The first humans corrupted one another and dragged down in their fall the entire creation whose masters they had been appointed.

If God allowed man to revolt in this way against himself, it was because he wanted his most perfect creature to exist in total freedom so that he could truly love his Creator ; for no love is genuine if it is not truly free. But man misused the freedom he had been granted in order to love God ; he made it serve his own self and so he fell into selfishness and pride, which sum up the full revolt of man against God, seeking to gain an impossible independence, obeying the urges of his own pleasure.

But God did not resign himself to the rebellion and fall of man. All through the course of history, he sought to restore the communion joining man to his love. The history of salvation is this long search culminating in the incarnation of the Son of God and the redemption of humanity by his death on the cross. There human sin is objectively and finally forgiven. But every human being who comes into this world, and is branded with the consequences of sin, who continually experiences within him and around him a rebirth of conditions of that initial sin, must, by faith, unite himself with Christ, who saved humanity on the cross, and so he can escape the consequences of the sin within him.

The mythical description of the original fall must bring us to reflect on our own personal history, in which we discover at the very source of our being, the same temptation to selfishness and pride, the same liking for independence and disobedience to God.

The human context into which we are born transmits sin to us and we readily consent to it. But God, who by the incarnation of the Son and the redemption on the cross has objectively and finally forgiven the sin of mankind, comes at the very beginning of our Christian lives, to grant us the effectual sign of his mercy : baptism. By baptism which plunges us into the love of Christ revealed on the cross, God drowns the destructive power of the original sin and grants us the power of the Holy Spirit, so that sin which is always springing up anew in us because we are part and parcel of humanity, should never become stronger than his grace, which saves us and holds us, until the very end of our lives, until the eternal Kingdom.

By baptism, that original sin, both historical and personal, is forgiven and drowned in every one of us ; we recover our original freedom to love God and the strength to fight and to conquer the powers of evil.

Our personal weakness is very often ready to yield to the temptations of the sinful world around which finds its resonance within us, but the power of the Holy Spirit, granted in baptism, gives us the possibility of true freedom with regard to sin, freedom to love God as he desired to be loved from the very creation of the world.

The Bible considers sin not only as personal offence against God and man, with its source in the heart and will of the individual, but also as the fruit of a temptation from outside. The Bible also considers evil as the work of external powers — the Bible calls them Satan, the devil or the demons — against which we must fight with spiritual weapons. Because Christ has conquered the powers of evil, the Christian can master them with the strength of the Holy Spirit within him.

11

ISRAEL

In his plan to snatch man and creation from the clutches of sin which was alienating them from him, God pursued his work of redeeming mankind, throughout history.

From the very beginning, the Creator allows sinful man to hope that one day the descendants of the woman will crush the head of the serpent, the power of evil (Gen. 3. 15). Abel, representing the first religious men, offered by faith a sacrifice pleasing to God, in spite of sin, and he was pronounced righteous by his Creator (Heb. 11. 4). Here we can see that, despite humanity's corruption, God sustained in men's hearts the desire to find him once more, and to be united with him by acts of sacrifice. After the symbolic account of the first murder, God put on Cain, the murderer, a sign of protection so that no one would strike him down (Gen. 4. 15). Then the Bible mentions the patriarch Enoch, who, by faith "walked with God" (Gen. 5. 24) and "pleased God" (Heb. 11. 5). His faith consisted essentially in believing that God exists and that he rewards those who search for him (Heb. 11. 6).

The mention of these personalities and their elementary relationship with God shows that the

Creator did not resign himself to sin but in his providence, sustained in man's heart a secret longing to recover his lost communion with himself.

The character of Noah then appears, one more symbol of mankind seeking after God and longing to obey him. The meaning of this mythological narrative is that God, throughout all the upheavals in this world, never varies in his love to mankind and in his desire to save his creatures, whom in justice he ought to destroy because they have rebelled against him. Noah is saved by faith and inherits the merciful justice of his Creator (Heb. 11.7). God makes a covenant with Noah, and in him with all living creatures and he gives them a sign of this covenant of peace : the rainbow, a reminder for God and for all living creatures that never again could any cosmic upheaval destroy creation, for it is the Creator's will to snatch them all from the clutches of sin (Gen. 9.12-17). So, Noah represents all mankind searching after God and he received in their name the assurance that God remembers every creature on earth and is leading each one into perfect peace with him and to that redemption which finds fulfilment in Christ.

One day Abraham is chosen by the Creator to receive the revelation of the one and only God and to become the representative of monotheistic religion which Jews, Christians and Muslims profess. In Abraham mankind is called to faith in the one God, against the deviations of polytheism, called to the obedience of faith which carries out the commands of God unconditionally. Abraham sets out, not knowing where God is leading him. He is willing to sacrifice his only son, the heir to all the promises. All the sons of Abraham, Jews, Christians and Muslims, find in him their father, a religious community of monotheistic faith and contemplative spirituality which accepts absolute obedience to God's commands whatever they are.

But Abraham is most particularly the father of the Jewish people who were to find one day in Moses their saviour and law-giver. Through Moses God takes the people of Israel out of Egypt and establishes them in the Promised Land, the place where his Word was to shine forth, and later be incarnate. In this way God chooses for himself a people which truly is the people of God, to whom he reveals his Word, gives his Law, and among whom he sets up signs of his presence : the Temple at Jerusalem and the liturgical worship offered there.

So Israel, the one and only people of God, becomes the witness of the Word of God among the nations. To Israel was entrusted the divine law and the spiritual worship desired and inspired by God. In this way the whole history of Israel becomes the history of the relationship of God and his people for the ultimate universal salvation of all mankind. The patriarchs, kings, priests and prophets become the bearers of the Word of the Lord for his people so that they are continually purified to be a light among the other nations. In spite of their faithlessness, rebellion and faults, God remains faithful to his people, as he promised Abraham and his descendants. He will never abandon Israel, never deny the covenant he made with them, for he has set his Word within them to enlighten the whole world.

God made Jerusalem, his holy city, and the Temple, in particular, the seat of his glory. There, God most high, eternal and almighty, revealed the real unseen presence of his glory, first of all under the sacred signs of the ark of the covenant, kept in the holy of holies, then under the sign of the empty space left in the sanctuary after the disappearance of the ark during Israel's exile in Babylon. The liturgy of word, psalms and sacrifices expressed their waiting in expectation of the Saviour-Messiah, for Israel, the light of the nations, was the place chosen in advance by God to reveal his presence one day, no longer in liturgical symbols, but in the reality of the existence of the Son, living among men.

Israel, the people chosen by God to enlighten the world, did not as a whole, recognize Jesus of Nazareth as its Messiah. Many of its sons, however, composed the Early Church, and for this we owe Israel our immense gratitude. Her theological, liturgical and spiritual tradition passed into the Church and adapted itself to the demands of the new preaching.

But besides all this, there is mystery in the refusal of Israel to recognize Jesus as the Messiah, a mystery guided by God himself. Thanks to this refusal the Gospel was heard by the whole world. Since they had been rejected by the Jewish authorities in Palestine, the apostles set out to bring the good news to the Jews dispersed throughout the Greco-Roman world and then to the pagans themselves. St. Paul makes it plain that the "fault of the Jews obtained the salvation of the non-Jews" (Rom. 11. 11) and that "their being set aside brought the the reconciliation of the world" (Rom. 11. 15). In fact, from every point of view, as Jesus said, "salvation comes from the Jews" (John 4. 22). Israel gave us the revelation of the Old Testament, the sonship of Abraham, into which the Saviour was born ; by its very refusal, the people of Israel rendered possible the reconciliation of the world ; and the Church was born in the theological, liturgical and spiritual tradition of Israel.

The Christians who are not members of the Jewish people are like branches of wild olive grafted on the original stem of the people of Israel. When the Jews accede to the faith, when all Israel and the Church are united, it will be like natural branches, being grafted afresh on the original olive tree. So the Church is closely related to Israel, the olive trunk originally chosen. The Gentile Christians in the Church, (those of non-Jewish origins), which includes most of us, are grafted against nature from the wild olive on the olive of Israel. The Judeo-Christians (of Jewish origin) for their part are grafted like natural branches on their own olive tree which has grown and spread into the world-Church (Rom. 11. 16-24). The unity of Israel, as a whole people, and the Church, will therefore be the ultimate fulfilment of Israel and the Church, who have a common destiny in the Kingdom of the Messiah, Jesus Christ.

12

THE INCARNATION

God, who is Love, could not resign himself to the rebellion and the estrangement of man. Israel and the prophets had been the preparation of his plan to reconcile humanity and all creation to himself. But this reconciliation was not possible for sinful man ; by himself he could not find the way back to his creator. Even God's messengers, because of their human limits and sinfulness, could not ensure man's complete liberation by their preaching of the Word of God. Their sinful humanity, in spite of the Word of God they bore, was still a screen too thick to allow that Word to be grasped in its full power of spiritual liberation. Someone without sin had to come and bring to mankind the power which frees him from the fetters of his rebellion and his sin, and reconciles him to God. Only his purity could permit all the rays of the divine grace to shine through. But this holy being had also to make salvation accessible to man. An angel he could not be, for his spirituality would have discouraged man and convinced him that what is possible for spiritual beings is not possible for flesh and blood. So it had to be someone holy, completely pure, and yet a man, completely human. So God, who alone is holy and pure decided to come himself, to live in our flesh and blood, and reconcile our humanity with himself.

If God was truly to share our humanity he could not simply live among us under an outward appearance of humanity. Then he too would have remained remote and we would not have felt involved with him, through his human example and his liberation of mankind. So God's will was to become man, he became a man like ourselves, except for sin. The person of the Son was incarnate in Jesus of Nazareth, the son of the Virgin Mary, according to the Father's will, by the action of the Holy Spirit.

The incarnation consisted in the indissoluble union of God the Son with a man absolutely identical with ourselves, but knowing no sin, holy and pure as he was, perfectly obedient to the Father and completely at the disposal of the Holy Spirit. Two distinct natures, human and divine, united in Mary at the time of the annunciation to her by the Angel. These two natures had to remain perfectly distinct during the time of the incarnation in order to ensure at one and the same time the real divinity and the complete humanity of the Son of God among us. But these two distinct natures found in the very person of the Son of God their true and perfect unity. Jesus Christ, son of God and son of Mary, is true God and true man, without confusion and without separation ; he is, in two distinct natures, divine and human, one single person : the eternal Son of God.

In this way God himself has shared our human condition in its entirety. For love of us, he came very near to us. He was a child, he experienced a child's wonderful joys and unspeakable sorrows. He was an adolescent, he knew the enthusiasms and passions of adolescence. He was a man, he experienced the happiness, the temptations, the distresses and the sufferings common to every human being.

He was loved and hated like any other man ; he knew human love and the disappointments human love can bring. He knew what it means to wait for death, alone and forsaken by many at the crucial hour. Christ really was myself, in all my humanity. So he can understand everything about my humanity of flesh and blood which he so perfectly shared.

The perfect communion of Christ-God with our humanity is the source of great joy for us. In Jesus-man we have a God who is intimately present and sympathetic ; in him we have the perfect friend who can understand everything and share everything, to whom we can tell everything and confide everything. Now nothing can separate us from this God-man who crossed the gap created by our rebellion and our sin. But, even if he is quite close to us, even if he is us in our humanity, in all his life he never knew sin ; his perfect holiness can sanctify us. His intimacy is not a sharing of our sinful state but of our humanity, for which it is possible not to sin. Through him, true man, we know and experience the intimacy of the God-Love, through him, the man of purity, we know and live the holiness possible to man.

In order to remain in the purity of the Christian faith, we must believe that Jesus Christ is the Son of God incarnate in our humanity, one single person in two natures, the divine and the human, neither being intermingled nor separated. If we see only the unity of the person of the Son of God, without affirming his two distinct natures, his divinity and his humanity, we make his incarnation of no avail, and the Lord remains a distant, inaccessible God. If we separate his two natures without considering the unity of the person of the Son of God, we run the risk of isolating his human nature, making Christ a prophet and forgetting he is God incarnate.

In Jesus Christ, God in the person of the Son became totally man, except for sin, while remaining totally God, in this marvellous incarnation.

13

THE VIRGIN MARY

To become man God chose to be born in the humblest and most obscure way by choosing as his mother a poor virgin.

Israel, as it waited for the promised Messiah, had often been represented symbolically as a woman, a virgin, the "daughter of Zion". God chose Mary to incorporate Israel's hope, as daughter of Zion. So when the Angel greets her on the day of the annunciation, he uses the messianic greeting, announcing the new age of deliverance. "Rejoice, in fullness of grace !"

God filled Mary with grace in order to prepare her to become his mother. This grace comes from God alone, in his love for mankind and for Mary. This unique grace sanctified Mary, not in order to remove her from the conditions of our humanity, but to strengthen her for the mystery of the incarnation which was to take place in her.

The fullness of God's grace comes to Mary in her poverty and her humility. In choosing a poor daughter of Israel, a virgin, in an obscure little country town, God makes his grace and his power shine forth in the very midst of human weakness and helplessness. Although Mary becomes the dwelling-place of God, she humbly considers herself the servant of the Lord.

Mary is called "mother of God" by the entire Christian tradition. The Council of Ephesus (in 431), which defined the title, wanted to affirm the total divinity of Christ and his total humanity. Jesus, the son of Mary mother of God, is truly God from the moment of his conception. If God, in his incarnation accepts a human mother, Mary, mother of God, it means that he has truly and totally become man.

Mary was to be the mother of the Messiah-King and this filled her with joy. She expressed her joy in the Magnificat, her hymn, in which she says that all generations will call her blessed, because the Lord has done great things for her. The Church sings this hymn, thanking God for Mary and proclaiming her blessed. Mary, together with all the saints, is present to the life of the Church and the Church joins with her in praising God.

Mary was also to be the mother of the Suffering Servant. In the temple on the day of the Presentation, Simeon prophesied to her : "A sword will pierce your own heart". In the course of the life of Jesus, Mary has to renounce her human motherhood gradually in order to become a member of the Body of Christ, the Church. She sees her son moving towards the tragic outcome of his ministry. Grief-stricken at the foot of the cross, she watches his fearful sufferings. And so, like every Christian, but still more painfully, because it was her own child who was dying, she makes up in her flesh, as St. Paul says, what was lacking in the sufferings of Christ. She was conformed to Christ crucified, and so she leads us on in our turn to be conformed to his sufferings so that we can know the joy of the resurrection. In this communion with Christ crucified, Mary's sufferings, like ours, become a prayer of intercession, the fervent offering of her whole life, that others too may know the happiness of perfect communion with Christ.

Mary is a figure of the Church. In her unique role as mother of the Son of God, Mary demonstrates to the Church its vocation to be a mother for the faithful : the Church gives birth to children of God, brothers and sisters of Christ, by the Word and by baptism : she nourishes them with this same Word and with the Eucharist ; she comforts them with absolution ; she leads them by the ministry of her pastors. Mary also shows the Church the way of service, poverty and humility, so that the glory of God and that alone may shine through her life. Mary is a spiritual mother in the Church, the first of the mothers a faithful disciple receives as reward for his obedience to the calling of God : "There is no one who leaves home, brothers, sisters, mother... for my sake and the gospel's who will not receive a hundred times more homes, brothers, sisters, mothers now at present..." The beloved disciple at the foot of the cross, symbolizing the believer, one of the brothers of Christ, received from Jesus on the cross, Mary, symbolizing the Church, as his mother. "Woman, here is your son — Son, here is your mother." Mary, a spiritual mother in the Church, invites us to receive the Church into our lives as our own mother, to love, to serve and to watch over.

In his vision of the Apocalypse, St. John saw the glorified Church in the guise of a woman in heaven ; and this woman has come to be identified with Mary. To look at Mary is to look at the Church moving on her way through the sufferings and the

conflicts of this world to the happiness of the Kingdom of God [6].

So we can pray :

"O Lord Christ, may we look to the cloud of
witnesses and find courage and strength for the
combats of this world ; accept their prayers, and
Mary's, united with ours in the communion of saints.
Grant that we may follow the example of faith,
devotion, constancy and holiness, of her who was
your human mother, and remains the figure of your
holy Church."

14

JESUS CHRIST, SON OF GOD

In the unique person of Jesus Christ, God came and lived our human life with all its difficulties, actually and in reality. In the people of Israel whom he had chosen from among all others to be his people, God had spoken, and given signs of his presence, through prophets and priests, in the sacred writings and in the sacrificial liturgies. But at the time of the incarnation he came himself, in person, to live among us, to rejoice, to suffer and to die as we do.

Our whole salvation lies in this complete participation in our life by God himself. Indeed, in spite of Word and signs, man was unable to recover a lasting communion with God. So God decided to become man to share in our existence completely and in this way to show us what it means to be truly human — to be fully in communion with God and one's fellow men. God really lived a human life, and herein lies the originality of the Christian faith, this being the event on which it is based.

Today, at every moment of his life, in every one of his joys, temptations, difficulties and sufferings, and on his way through death, man can tell himself

that God in Christ has already experienced that. He
rejoiced, he endured the very same difficulties and
sufferings, he too knew agony and death. Everywhere and always, in all circumstances, Christ, God
and man, is with us. And in this total communion
with God's humanity, in God's union with our
humanity, we discover the possibility of our
salvation — conformity with the life of Christ,
participation in his death and a sharing in his
victory.

Our whole spiritual life consists in looking at
Christ, contemplating Christ in himself and in every
one of our brothers and sisters. Contemplation and
brotherly love are closely linked. We meet Christ in
contemplation and in him every one of our fellows.
In brotherly love we meet our brothers, and in them
the living Christ. Our faith and our prayers are not
directed to a distant and inaccessible God. God is
indeed transcendent, that is to say he is distinct
from his creatures. Christianity is not a pantheism
which sees God compounded and intermingled with
all that is created. And yet the transcendence and
the personality of God which make him distinct
from creation and from us, do not make him a
distant, hidden God. Ever since he lived among us
in his incarnation, God has stayed close to us. We
find him very near in his Word, in his sacraments,
and in our brothers. In our sisters and brothers we
see the face of Christ.

Brotherly love or charity is not an effort separate
from loving God or from believing. Loving God and
loving our neighbour is one and the same thing.
When, for example, St. Paul exhorts us to weep with
those who weep or to rejoice with those who rejoice,
he is inviting us to a communion of human feelings,
but also to recognize in the suffering of a brother,
the very suffering of Christ, or, in his joys the

presence of the risen Christ. Weeping with a brother or sister in sorrow is to stand at the foot of Christ's cross and perceive the suffering of the Crucified in our neighbour's heart. In the contemplation of Christ by prayer, meditation and the Eucharist, we find our brothers and sisters, and our love for them is renewed. In loving we contemplate the face of Christ, crucified and risen again, completely human in all our troubles and our joys, and our love for him burns stronger.

Throughout his life on earth, the Son of God, Jesus Christ manifested himself as Messiah and prophet ; in his death he manifested himself as Mediator and priest ; in his resurrection, as Lord and King.

While he was alive Christ showed by his words, by his miracles, and by his whole life of love and sacrifice, that he truly was the Messiah, the liberator for whom the people of Israel had been waiting. He showed that he was the perfect prophet who has the words of life and whose touch restores life. In dying, Christ became our one and only Mediator, the one who alone, by his total self-giving, could restore the lost communion between man and God. He was the perfect priest, offering the perfect sacrifice, his own body, to restore our union with God. By his resurrection, he won the greatest victory in history, the victory over death, so becoming for everyone of us the hope of a resurrection like his. He became the Lord and King of the universe to whom all powers are subject, and who leads his Church infallibly, and with her the whole creation, to the eternal glory of the Kingdom of God.

15

LIBERATION

It was by his entire life among us that Christ revealed his love, but this revelation was accomplished supremely in the sacrifice he made of himself by dying on the cross.

The *redemption* of humanity by Christ is the act by which he rescued mankind from the power of evil ; this act was his entire earthly life, but most particularly his death on the cross. Redemption means ransom, buying back again. The image conveyed by this word means that man is as it were sold to sin, selfishness, pride and greed. So Christ came to ransom him, to rescue him from those evil powers, and the ransom price he paid was the sacrifice on the cross. If he was to offer man a possible way out, liberation from those powers estranging us from God, Christ had to stay true to the very end in his conformity, participation and fellowship with man : he shared in everything we experience, except sin. Indeed, he had to be as completely human as we are, in order to show us how we could be truly human ; but he had to be without sin, because sin disfigures our human nature ; if he had known sin, he would not have been able to help us out of it.

This redemption, this ransom, this rescue of man from the powers of evil is accomplished in a complete *substitution* of Christ for our human nature. We were not able to extricate ourselves ; all our efforts, even when directed by moral and religious law, were quickly exhausted, so completely was our will captive to the powers of evil. It was not possible for man to save himself, even by trying to obey God. Because of his weakness, man could never climb up again to God, from whom sin had torn him. Since man could not take even one step back towards God, without soon slipping back and falling again, God resolved to descend into the depths of his misery. Christ put himself in man's place completely, so that he could grasp him by the hand and walk with him on the road back to God. Our whole salvation consists of this total substitution of Christ ; he has really taken our place. However deep we fall into human suffering and distress, we find Christ beside us to rescue us from the clutches of despair. The slightest stirring of readiness to begin to believe in God and to obey him, is brought about in us by him. Since he identified himself with us so perfectly, we are able to say continually in all times of distress or of hope : Christ is my life, it is no longer I who live, Christ lives in me.

He substituted himself for man even in death itself, and death on the cross. And in this most terrible of deaths, the death of a robber, outcast and condemned, he effected the *expiation* of our sin. This expiation should be understood in the sense of the substitution of Christ for our sinful human nature and in the sense of the fellowship of Christ with all our human misery. Because of our estrangement from God, our rebellion against him and our refusal to obey his word of life, we have deserved condemnation and abandonment by God. But God is love : he refused to let himself be affected by our ingratitude and our sin. He came himself in the person of his Son, in Jesus Christ, to rescue us from the vicious circle of our rebellion against his will. And Christ died on the cross like a criminal, he who was good. As we contemplate the Crucified, we appreciate the seriousness of our fault which deserved such a punishment ; and yet God spares us this condemnation and this punishment. However, we have to realize the inevitable end of our sinful life and that is why he makes it plain to us in the person of Christ crucified, who became the condemned criminal in our place, he who was sinless. He alone is able to endure this punishment, without rebelling and without hating God. There, at the foot of the cross, we plumb the depths of our ingratitude to God, and we are constrained to fall down in an act of profound repentance. But at the same time, because it is the love of God himself, sacrificing himself, we are raised up in thanksgiving and adoration. We adore the Crucified who accepts this death in our place, in order to reveal our sin to us, we thank him for his boundless love, sacrificing itself for us and enduring to the very end. And it is in this mystery of the sacrifice of the cross, revealing simultaneously our sin and God's love, that we are drawn by Christ and restored to perfect communion with the Father. In this act of Christ's love totally sacrificed for us, our salvation is accomplished with the recovery of our communion with God. Nothing can ever separate us now from the love of God made manifest in Jesus Christ.

This redemption, this substitution, this expiation, is accomplished for all ; those contemporary with Christ, all who are yet unborn and also all who preceded him in time. The Gospel was also preached to the dead, for Christ descended into the dwelling of the dead. This brief mention in the sacred texts does not allow us to write at length on this mystery, but it is enough to give us comfort.

There is a place where all who never had the occasion on this earth of meeting Christ, can have this decisive confrontation. How can we imagine this place ? Is it even possible ? Enough for us to know that in another life, all non-Christians can have a new chance of salvation through Christ. By descending into the dwelling of the dead, the Saviour revealed this incredible promise ; every man, in this life, or in another, can decide for Christ or against him [7]. Salvation is truly universal.

16

RESURRECTION

Once he has lived a complete human destiny, from birth to the grave, the Son of God wins the resurrection victory, the first act in a new era, the era of the resurrection to life eternal of all who bind themselves to him, in faith, hope and love. By his resurrection, Christ bears the whole of humanity with him in a movement of radical renewal. By the power of his resurrection, the Church begins to perform miracles : changing lives, giving new hearts, and even healing bodies.

At the moment when Christ's truly dead body woke up to life, on Easter morning, a radical upheaval occurred in human nature, indeed in all creation. The human body until then had been the restricting form of the human person ; now it became the real and visible vehicle of eternal being, able to move about and to pass through material obstacles, having no limitations whatever. The visible body of the Risen Christ gives us a glimpse of the promise of that body which will guarantee us life, real, yet without limitations, throughout the whole eternity of the Kingdom of God.

But Christ's resurrection does not only produce

a miraculous effect on human nature. The whole created order is made new, as if brought into a new creation. The supernatural energies unleashed by the cosmic explosion of Christ's resurrection affect the whole created universe. The resurrection of Christ could be compared to a tremendous atomic explosion progressively affecting all the elements of creation, leaving absolutely nothing intact, an explosion which is not destructive and disintegrating, but which orders and reintegrates. So the resurrection of Christ, breaking with the natural order of fallen creation, reaches the very heart of all creatures by its power, inspiring them with the life-giving Spirit who effects new creation. This process by which creation is renewed through the power of the resurrection, works progressively, being destined to find its perfect fulfilment in the Kingdom. St. Paul, speaking of Christians who have the first fruits of the Spirit, says that all creation is groaning in the labour of new birth.

Through the resurrection, which has renewed the whole creation, all the elements of this world find a meaning again, being directed towards the glory of the Kingdom. All the elements of creation are converging to fulfilment, by the power of Christ's resurrection restoring and reorganising the whole universe.

That is why, for the Church and for the Christian, nothing on this earth can be a matter of indifference or contempt. The spiritual life does not mean separating oneself from the created world ; it involves discerning there a hidden work of the Risen Christ, in order to offer it in praise to God. So we contribute to the progressive liberation of creation from its slavery to sin, and to the entry of every creature into the eternal Kingdom. There is a profoundly cosmic quality in the resurrection which transfigures nature.

By the resurrection, Christ is established Lord over the world. He rules invisibly but actually, over every power and every wisdom of this world. As they proclaim the universal lordship of Christ, the Church and the Christian try to discern the signs of his presence wherever they are manifest. Of course, the truth about God, Christian theological knowledge, can only be discovered in the revelation of the Word of God, in the Scriptures known and interpreted by the Church through her entire tradi- tion. But the Lord Christ is master of the world, directing all power and all wisdom. So truth may be found wherever the Lord wills to reveal it. To be sure, the touchstone of truth will be the Word of God alone ; but the Church must always rejoice in truth, beauty and goodness, wherever she discovers them.

The lordship of Christ obliges the Church to be profoundly optimistic regarding the world, science, philosophy, religion and even politics. The risen and glorious Christ reigns over all things and it can be his will that men's strivings in science, philosophy, religion and politics, should reveal facets of the truth and work to the glory of God. Enlightened by the Word of God and enlivened by the optimism of the lordship of Christ, the Church is alert and watchful to discern truth, beauty and goodness wherever they are to be found, in order to direct them on towards that fullness which is in the whole truth : Jesus Christ. When a fire is burning at night, sparks can be seen isolated in the darkness. Although the sparks are separated from the flames, they have come none the less from the fire itself. So it is with the elements of truth scattered throughout the world. They can only have come from Jesus Christ, the source of all truth.

Christ Wisdom, the risen and glorious Lord, who directs all thinking, himself guides the research of scientists and scholars, allowing them gradually to make discoveries which can increase our knowledge and our joy. They can, of course, misuse these gifts of God, but that detracts in no wise from their values as manifestations of the truth which is in Jesus Christ, the source of all truth.

Christ the Master also directs the wisdom of philosophers and allows them to organize the discoveries of men into a synthesis glorifying the wisdom of the Creator of all things.

Christ the Lord is also behind the religious gropings of men who do not know him, of non-Christian ascetics who are seeking to submit their lives to the spirit. He gives them access to the contemplation of God and prepares them to receive love in its fullness, which is himself. He supports them in their spiritual life and their moral living. He accepts their worship, even if it is elementary, and grants them spiritual communion in which they receive a provisional joy, a preparation for the joy of perfect communion in the Eucharist.

Christ the King conducts world politics despite all the devious ways of its interests and its passions. He allows the leaders of governments to do only what is not inconsistent with the direction of history as he is guiding it. Unknown to them and unrecognised by them, he frequently enlightens them in decisions for the good of all mankind.

One day, at the end of time, we shall reread the history of the world in the light of Christ, and understand all that he inspired and directed in his omnipotence and omniscience as universal Lord.

17

ASCENSION

His life on earth completed, Christ took with him the humanity of his risen body, acquired in the incarnation. So we are truly represented in God himself ; God has been enriched by having shared the experience of our human life.

The ascension of Christ signifies the presence of our humanity in God, the assumption of the human into divinity. So we have a representative and an intercessor with the Father.

Christ is our high priest who unites our praises and our prayers in his praise and his prayer ; he presents them to the Father who hears us and blesses us. All our aspirations, our expectations and our requests pass through the Son to be purified in him and presented to the Father of lights.

The Son is present in the Trinity bearing the marks of his redeeming passion. He is a living and eternal reminder of all he accomplished once and for all upon the cross ; and this is an effectual prayer before the Father for all our needs. At the same time that he is a living memorial before the Father of his redeeming sacrifice, he unites in his intercession all our praises and all our supplications, which the Father answers by granting us through him and in him all the graces and the blessings we need to live faithfully and joyously.

In his ascension Christ bears with him all the possible values of our humanity ; through him and in him the Father brings these values to their fulfilment. So it is in union with Christ glorified, by contemplation and prayer, that we can hope for the transfiguration of our personal humanity and of humanity collectively. Christ takes upon himself all our difficulties and our sufferings and transfigures them, to fill us with joy and love. He also takes into himself all the values of our humanity to fulfil them, perfect and transfigure them into the fullness of truth, beauty and goodness found in himself alone.

Our life then, is hidden with Christ in God. Our Christian existence is a continual communion with Christ, as we know him in his earthly life and as he is in God, glorious in his glorified humanity. It is also an expectation of his return ; for Christ, as he returned to the Father, bearing our humanity, will come gloriously at the end of the world to make manifest his universal lordship for all to see. We await this return peacefully and pray to God to hasten this end and the visible establishment of his Kingdom. Only then shall we see in all its fullness what we now believe — Christ the King, Lord of all the universe, directing and ordering all things and leading on to their final fulfilment all the truth, beauty and goodness that our humanity contains, in spite of the sin that obscures it. Then, as the Revelation puts it, all the riches of the nations will enter into the Kingdom, and, transfigured, sing their Creator's glory.

18

THE HOLY SPIRIT

The Risen Christ, established as universal Lord through his ascension, did not intend to leave the Christians orphaned. At Pentecost he sends the Holy Spirit upon the disciples as he promised. The Holy Spirit, the third person of God-Trinity, inaugurates a new age for the people of God. Before the incarnation he had manifested himself intermittently, raising up prophets, inspiring wise men and guiding heroes of the faith. With Christ, God drew very near to man, accompanying him through all his earthly journey. But that incarnate presence of God was bound to be restricted to one place and one time. However, after this unique incarnation, God does not mean to cease being intimately present with man. On the contrary, he means to continue his presence, limited in Jesus Christ incarnate, under another mode, by the Holy Spirit — universally present to all, intimately present with each one. By the Holy Spirit every one who accepts faith in Christ and receives baptism is established in a unique relationship with God. God is perpetually beside him ; God permeates his whole being and his whole life ; God comes to dwell in him ; his body becomes the temple of the Holy Spirit.

This mysterious presence of God within each Christian cannot be explained. Yet it is a fundamental of the faith, that by the Holy Spirit, God, who is present everywhere, can live within anyone who believes in Christ as his Saviour. So we understand why Christ told his apostles that it was better for them that he should go away, that the unique but restricted age of the incarnation should come to an end. Indeed the local presence of God incarnate in Jesus Christ, has become, by the gift of the Holy Spirit at Pentecost, a universal, inner presence. The Holy Spirit lives in the whole Church and in each member of the Church.

The indwelling of the Holy Spirit in the Church and in the individual Chrsitian does not imply a confusion of the divine with the created. The person of the Holy Spirit does not absorb human personality. Man remains a created being, a creature who can be tempted to sin, to disobey God. But the Holy Spirit is there, present, ready to transfigure each Christian person, sanctifying him and leading him to life eternal. The Holy Spirit manifests the faithfulness of God for anyone who really wants to be his, in spite of infidelities. The Holy Spirit is with us for ever.

The Holy Spirit, whom the Father gives and sends is "the other Paraclete". This means that just like Christ himself, he too is our guide and counsellor, our helper and comforter, our advocate and our defender.

As Christ promised, the Holy Spirit was to recall to the disciples all he had told them ; he was to inspire them and guide them in founding the Church through faith in the gospel. This inspiration of the apostles by the Holy Spirit, recalling the revelation received, becomes in the Church an aid to interpret this revelation and to apply it to the needs of the people of God. The Holy Spirit guides the Church into all truth ; he it is who effects in her the development of her understanding of revealed truth. The Holy Spirit does not speak on his own authority ; he does not bring a new revelation to the Church but in the heart of the Church he tells how she is to understand the eternal Gospel of Christ. He can also foretell future events and so give the Church a true vision of historical events.

The Holy Spirit is the guide and counsellor of every individual Christian. He directs each one in life and enlightens him so that he discovers his vocation and God's will for him. We have to be aware of the presence of the Holy Spirit close by us and often ask him for his guidance and his light to direct our lives and to help us come to decisions.

The Holy Spirit is also also our helper and our comforter. In the difficulties and troubles of life he supports and comforts us, he revives our courage whenever it may flag. In the life of prayer the Holy Spirit is particularly active to comfort and help. The Holy Spirit comes to help us in our weakness ; for we do not know how we ought pray, but the Spirit himself intercedes for us in sighs too deep for words. So, in St. Paul's thinking, the Holy Spirit assists us in our spiritual life and in our prayers. He puts into our hearts the desire for contemplation and the very words of our intercessions. The Holy Spirit also assists our faith, our hope and our charity. He strengthens us when doubts bring us low ; he sends his light into hearts always threatened by darkness. He gives us a foretaste of life eternal and so revives our hope when all the despair of this world might destroy it. He rekindles within us the fire of God's love for men so that we can love with hearts ready for compassion and for sacrifice. If anyone falls I burn, aflame with the fire of love kindled by the Holy Spirit.

The Holy Spirit is the advocate and defender of the Church and of each one of her members. Wherever the world tries to annihilate the Gospel, the Holy Spirit comes to help the Church and Christians, giving them words for their defence. The Christian can confront a hostile world in perfect peace ; he has no need to spend a long time preparing his defence ; he needs only to submit himself in love to the aid of the Holy Spirit who will put into his heart and on his tongue the words he has to speak.

The Holy Spirit, who was sent down upon the newborn Church, is always invoked by her on everything she performs in her ministry. The Church invokes the Holy Spirit on every Christian at baptism, that God may dwell in him and guide him in faith, hope, love and prayer. She invokes the Holy Spirit as she confirms Christians in faith, witness and service. She invokes him upon the bread and the wine of the Eucharist, so that the Holy Spirit may fulfil the words of the Lord, that this bread and wine may become the body and blood of Christ, really present. The Church invokes the Holy Spirit on Christians who confess their sins, that they may be purified and comforted. She invokes him upon the sick, that they may be strengthened. She invokes him at each wedding, that the marriage may be faithful and indissoluble ; upon nuns and monks that they may be made strong in their vocation and live joyfully their vows of community, celibacy and obedience. The Church invokes the Holy Spirit upon all her ministers, that they may faithfully proclaim the word of truth and administer the sacraments as instituted by Christ, leading the people of God as true shepherds of the flock entrusted to them.

In all that she does the Church lives by the Holy Spirit and invokes his powerful aid. Through him she consecrates all mankind and the whole creation, that the world may become an offering, to the praise of its Creator and its Saviour.

19

THE CHURCH

The Church is the community, local and universal, of those people who have adhered to Christ by faith and baptism, and who desire to persevere in a life nourished by the Word of God and the sacraments, consecrated to the witness and service of the Gospel in charity. The Church continues the work of Christ on earth : having been instituted by him, she is the instrument of the Word of God in the world.

The Church is prefigured in Israel, the people of God, and it is essential for her to keep a close link of communion and solidarity with that people. Christ founded the Church within the people of Israel, so the unity of the Church and Israel should be sought as the normal situation willed by God for his people.

The Church was founded by Christ in three major stages. First of all Jesus gathered around him his twelve apostles to be witnesses of his life on earth, of his death and his resurrection. This group, or body, of the Twelve is the nucleus of the Church, as a people in continuity with Israel, which was made up of twelve tribes, and as an institution which transmits the Word of Christ with the sacraments of his presence and his work. The Twelve represent both the Church considered as a whole people, the laity (from *laos* — people), and the Church as an institution, the ministry ; all the laity and all the ministers of the Church are present in the Apostles. Then, at the foot of the cross, the Church was born of the Spirit of the Crucified and the blood shed for the redemption of humanity. There the Church appeared in the figure of Mary, as the Mother of all the disciples loved by Christ, symbolized in St. John. Finally, the Church was manifested at Pentecost, in the power of the Holy Spirit, with her universal mission. So the Church was founded by Christ as an apostolic body, as mother of the faithful and as instrument of the Holy Spirit for the proclamation of the Gospel throughout the world.

The Church, as the instrument of the Word of God on earth does not exist for herself, but for the world. She is not a fortress in which to enclose oneself and live a life of security, the better to fight the enemy. The Church is a consecrated people spread throughout the world, sent to seek out the seed which Christ, the universal Lord, has already sown abundantly over all the earth ; she helps this seed to grow by the radiance of the light of the Holy Spirit and by the warmth of supernatural love. She rejoices in all the signs of the work of Christ which she encounters in the world, all truth, all beauty and all goodness ; she encourages the growth of these human values, fruits of the hidden action of God, in order to bring them to the perfect maturity of the Kingdom, by the light of the Gospel and the consecration of the sacraments ; all these values the Church offers to the praise of God in the thanksgiving of the Eucharist.

The Church *(ecclesia)* is the assembly of the people of God. God alone knows his whole people in their entirety. There is a mystery of the Church, the people of God, which transcends the ecclesiastical institution, overflowing the boundaries of the Church of the baptised, built and structured by the ministries. There is a close bond between the Church, the people of God, known to God alone, and the Church, the institution of liberation through the Gospel and the sacraments ; the second is the sign of the first.

The Word of God, living (Christ) ; written (the Bible) ; and preached (the proclamation of the Church), gathers the Church ; the baptism of water and Spirit incorporates men in the Church ; the Eucharist nourishes and structures the Church ; the ministry governs the Church and preserves her in unity.

All who are baptised are part of the Church, but she also includes potentially all the people Christ is secretly preparing for the revelation of his love. So the Church is far wider and more numerous than is apparent to the eyes of the world. She is the people known to God in his love.

The Church is the Body of Christ. The phrase is not only an analogy. It expresses a profound reality. At the cross all the people of God were met in one truly obedient man, Christ crucified, closely linked with his mother, the Virgin Mary, and St. John, the disciple whom Jesus loved, the first fruits of the New Covenant. At Pentecost the Body of Christ expands from the nucleus of the body of the apostles, by the power of the Holy Spirit ; and it will never cease to grow as a visible universal assembly, the actual manifestation on earth of the humanity of Jesus Christ.

The Body of Christ is the Church, as a visible organism in the service of its Lord, the instrument of his living Word, turned towards the world and expressing itself in organised ministries.

The Church, the Body of Christ, is a tangible

reality, visible, organised, structured and manifested, locally and universally.

The Church is also the Bride of Christ ; this implies that she is not simply an organism structured by organised ministries, not only a body or an institution, but a person enjoying a special relationship with her Lord. Like Mary of Bethany, the Church is at the feet of Christ in an attitude of adoration and contemplation. She is not only the servant of God for action in the world, she is also called to express the prayer, praise and worship of Christians, of all believers and of the whole creation in its aspiring to God. The Church then has not only a provisional active role until Christ returns, but also a definitive contemplative role, because she will finally appear in the Kingdom of God.

The Church, as the Bride of Christ, is called to a life of sanctification. She cannot be subject to the realities of this world, she is completely orientated towards the coming Kingdom of God which she proclaims in word and in deed ; every day she awaits the glorious return of Christ, her Lord ; she expresses this expectancy most particulary in her liturgy. The Church can have no other attitude towards all human power and wealth than that of detachment and freedom. The Church, the Bride of Christ, is a servant Church, a poor Church, in an attitude of total dependence upon her Master, who alone can change her poverty into fullness.

The Church is one, holy, catholic or universal, and apostolic.

As the instrument of the Word of God on earth, as the assembly of the people of God, as the Body of Christ and as the Bride of Christ, the Church is one. All the baptised are incorporated in a single people and in a single body, to witness to their one and only Saviour. The Church is the one and only

Bride of Christ. She contemplates him and serves him in her universal liturgy, in the rich diversity of its expressions. The unity of all the baptised has also to show itself visibly in the unity of the fundamental faith and the sacramental life. Unfortunately, through the fault of men, the visible unity of the Church has been compromised in history [8]. The ecumenical movement, which is now alive in every part of Christendom, tends towards the restoration of this visible unity of faith and sacraments, in one single Church. This unity does not imply uniformity, but an organic bond of unity between all the local Churches in their valid diversities, so that all the baptised, confessing the same faith, are able to share together in the same sacraments, in particular the same Eucharist, the sign of their unity in the Body of Christ.

The Church is holy, because the Holy Spirit dwells in her and she is sanctified by the good deposit of Word and sacraments. She is a holy institution, because of the holy words she proclaims and the holy acts she performs, and also a community of sinners, but sinners who are constantly being forgiven. We must make a distinction in the Church between the sacred functions such as preaching, liturgy and sacraments, and the persons who perform them ; we have to make a distinction between the holy ministry of Word and sacraments, and the sinful persons who exercise that holy ministry. The holiness of the Church which signifies the faithfulness of God towards his people implies indefectibility : the gates of hell will not prevail against her ; the Church can compromise neither fundamental Christian belief nor her sacramental life. Even at the darkest times in the Church's history, Christ preserves the essence of her ministry for the salvation of men [9].

The Church is universal or catholic, because it is in her that the fullness of Christ can be attained on this earth. This fullness is firstly fullness of truth ; it is in the Church universal that the greatest fullness of truth possible in this world is to be found ; the judgment of the universal Church is fullness of truth as compared with the judgment of the individual or of the local Church. The fullness of the Church comes to her in her immense diversity from which she embodies the spiritual experience of all men in space and in time ; this fullness of the universal Church reduces nationalisms or recent particular traditions to proper perspective. The fullness of the universal Church is a fullness of life ; in the life of the Church a man's whole being is enlisted for the worship and the service of God ; this fullness of life can be seen in the Christian liturgy and in Christian ethics, both of which demand the participation of our entire being and the whole creation to the glory of God. The Church is universal, catholic or "fullness", because in her the particular is set in the totality : in fullness of truth, of space, of time and of life.

The Church is apostolic because she recognizes her fundamental identity with the Church of Christ's apostles, as seen in Holy Scripture. The Church is apostolic because of her faithfulness to Holy Scripture, understood in the spirit of the apostolic tradition throughout the centuries ; she is apostolic by her celebration of the sacraments instituted by Christ and celebrated by the apostles ; she is apostolic by the continuity of her ministry in the service of Christ [10]. She is apostolic because she is missionary and because, until Christ returns in glory, she will not cease to proclaim the Gospel to all men.

20

THE COMMUNION OF SAINTS

The Church is the visible community of Christians, which opens and trains them to an invisible communion, the communion of the saints. We have already seen that the Church, conceived as the community of the baptised, built and structured by the ministries is far outpassed and exceeded by the Church conceived as the people of God, known to him alone. But there is a still greater extension of the Church : the communion of saints, uniting together all the faithful of every time and place. The Church, as a visible, universal community, bears along with her a vast people known to God alone ; she is surrounded by the great cloud of witnesses from every time and place, living with Christ and awaiting the glorious manifestation of the Kingdom of God.

The communion of saints is the vast community of all the faithful on earth, known or unknown to the visible Church, and because of the death of the body, of all the faithful in the unseen, called by the Bible heaven or paradise. The communion of saints is also the hidden spiritual bond, uniting the faithful of every age and place in one fellowship of prayer, life, joy and suffering. This bond is none other than the work of the Holy Spirit, uniting all the members of the Body of Christ, all who are part of the march of the people of God, all the faithful on earth and in paradise, people of every time and place.

The communion of saints is a solidarity in prayer. All who belong to Christ by faith and baptism uphold one another with prayers of intercession, praying for one another. When death comes, this bond of prayer is not broken. Christian tradition believes that those who have left us for the unseen life with God, continue to include us in their prayers, and so they help us in their intercessions to the Father [11]. It is Christ, our great high priest, who presides over this great universal prayer of all Christians, gathers it up and offers it to the Father in his supreme intercession.

The communion of saints is also a solidarity in life, joy and suffering. All Christ's faithful people are united in one common universal life. They can be examples for one another. If one member of Christ's body is joyful, all the members rejoice with him ; if one members suffers, all the members suffer with him. And so our lives, our joys and our sufferings can be offered to God in prayer and bear fruit in the lives of others. Our joy can bring others to glorify God ; our sufferings can help someone else in difficulty. This is the greatest hope and the greatest support for a Christian in illness or sorrow.

The lives, joy and suffering of those who have gone before us and are now at rest with God, have the same power of example, attracting and offering. That is why the Church chooses members of the Body of Christ who have been particulary exemplary witnesses, to be remembered by Christians for their encouragement. It is the memory of the saints who symbolize by their lives, their faith and their obedience that spiritual treasury formed by all those who are united in the communion of all the saints, that is to say, all Christians everywhere and through-out all the ages. The Church remembers in her liturgy the Virgin Mary, John the Baptist, the apostles, the martyrs and all the principal witnesses in her history. She offers them as examples of faith and of life ; she recalls their present prayers before the Father ; she unites us with them in the great pro-cession of Christians, journeying on towards the Kingdom of God.

This memorial of the saints recalls before God what these witnesses have done for his service and his glory. It recalls their offering, and their prayers so that he may answer them and grant us a share in their blessing. So among all the faithful there is this wonderful exchange of the communion of saints, which allows us all to share together in the treasury of blessings which the Lord has poured out century by century in all those who are his, who pray to him, live, rejoice and suffer for him.

It is through the Word of God which makes us know and love Christ, through the sacraments which make Christ's presence and his action real to us, that we have access to the communion of saints, for we have no direct communion with them or they with us, only through Christ, and in him. The unity and communion of all the faithful is only possible in Christ and by the action of the Holy Spirit. It is, then, by the ministry of Christ, accomplished through the Church and in the power of the Holy Spirit, that we can benefit by the treasures of the communion of saints. The Apostles' Creed indicates this ministry of Christ in the Church when it refers to the remis-sion of sins. We shall see later how this ministry is performed and in what various ways. As sin hinders our communion with God, it is by sin's remission, through God's mercy, that this communion is res-tored and that God regards us as saints, sinners completely forgiven, and makes us share in the blessings of the communion of saints.

21

ETERNAL LIFE

All who are united with Christ by faith and baptism, who have been nourished by the gospel and the Eucharist and have so persevered in love for God and their neighbours, are promised the resurrection of their whole being into eternal life. Christ made that promise clear : "It is my Father's will that everyone who sees the Son and believes in him should have eternal life, and I will raise him again on the last day... Anyone who believes has eternal life... Anyone who eats my flesh and drinks my blood has eternal life and I will raise him up at the last day." Faith in Christ and communion at the Eucharist convey the promise of resurrection.

A Christian has within himself new life which will never end. He will always have life with Christ. The physical death of a Christian intervenes and changes the course of this eternal life. From being visible in the body, he passes to the unseen (for human beings) of life with God, but he does not cease to be alive, in Christ by the power of the Holy Spirit. Paradise, or heaven, is the name given to this unseen life of the faithful who have died and are with God, the same eternal life they received here on earth in faith and in the sacraments, which continues in the unseen. This place, or time, called paradise, is rest in the vision of God and the communion of saints. It does not exclude activity in prayer and mutual help between the faithful who have died and those who are still waging the battle of life on earth. This unseen life is perfect happiness in the peace of God.

The Scriptures give us glimpses of another home, another time or another life, where all who have never had the chance on earth of real encounter with Christ or of consciously committing themselves to him, have another chance to believe and to be saved. The Apostles' Creed calls it "hell", "the dwelling of the dead". But the Christian revelation remains very discreet about the other life. It only indicates enough to comfort us about the fate of those who die without knowing Christ, and to show the universality of the gospel which was, and is, preached even to the dead [12].

The Bible also speaks of a third possibility after death : hell and damnation. Anyone who has really known Christ, been united with him by faith, received the sacraments, benefited from the graces of the Holy Spirit, and, realizing fully what he is doing, rejects salvation, to some degree crucifies Christ afresh, and blasphemes against the Holy Spirit. For this blasphemy against the Holy Spirit there is no forgiveness possible, either in this world or the next. It is difficult to imagine the possibility of such situation. The Scriptures do, however, mention it as a warning. For a Christian there is the possibility of the ultimate sin, blasphemy against the Holy Spirit, categorical expulsion from one's heart of the Spirit's presence and activity. This possible sin against the Holy Spirit, this conscious, wilful rejection of the Christian faith and the Christian life, leads to condemnation with no pardon possible. Since God respects our freedom, he leaves us free to refuse him, knowing full well what we are doing. This situation, difficult to imagine, but possible nevertheless, leads to separation from God. This separation and forgetting is called hell or damnation. Anyone who has willed this state of affairs, experiences a second death, death not only of the body, but of the spirit. He is no longer worthy of living before God. He lapses into nothingness. Obviously it is not possible for anyone, nor for the Church, to pass such a judgment on anybody, however low he may have fallen. God alone knows if such people exist and who they are [13].

When God judges that the Church's time for preaching the Gospel to the ends of the earth is completed, Christ will come, visibly and gloriously, to bring the world as we know it to an end. No one knows the day or the hour of this end or of this return. The apostles did not know and they may have supposed that Christ's return was imminent. When he was incarnate, the Son of God himself did not reveal it. This secret of God and this ignorance of the Church are necessary to keep our expectation continuous and alert. Every day, the Church and Christians must be ready to welcome Christ returning in his glory.

With this glorious return of Christ, universal resurrection will take place. All who are alive on earth will see their bodies transformed as was the Risen Christ's. All in the unseen realm of physical death will reappear in the visible form of a resurrection body. This glorious body which will allow us all to see each other again, should be conceived as being like the body of Christ after his resurrection. It will be a visible, tangible body, but free from its present handicaps of matter, sin and sickness. This glorious new body will express each one's personality in its perfection of beauty.

And then, the transfiguration of all creation

will follow. The whole created world will attain perfection, so that we will be able to speak of new heavens and a new earth. God will set up his Kingdom, and, in the perfection of this renewed creation, we will be able to lead an eternal life of bliss, free from sin, free from sickness, sadness and death. All our desires as beloved creatures of God will be fulfilled, in joy and in peace.

The Way

22

GOD'S WORD AND SACRAMENTS

It is through the reading and proclaiming of the word of God in the Holy Scriptures, and through the sacraments, that the Holy Spirit awakens faith in our hearts and effects our sanctification.

God comes to us in the mystery of our life and in the secret work of his Spirit within us. The work of God in us and in the world cannot be confined to his word and sacraments. However, although it is beyond question that God is acting invisibly and secretly in people and in the world by his providence and his mercy, we know the means of grace through which he acts visibly and explicitly; they are his word and the sacraments of his presence and his working. As we read or as we listen to the proclamation of his word, it is God himself we hear, speaking to us, calling us and directing our ways. In the sacraments, it is God himself who acts : such is the meaning he himself has given to these actions performed by the Church. Although the activity of God is universal, far exceeding the reach of his word and his sacraments, it is in them that we can be sure of hearing him and meeting him.

The proclamation of God's word in the reading of Holy Scripture makes it possible for us to hear

God himself. This is an undoubted reality for Christian believers and yet it is a profound mystery. Since Holy Scripture contains the facts of the history of salvation — the relationship between God and humanity — since it contains the words spoken by God through his prophets, directly by Christ and afterwards through his apostles, the reading of its text and the proclamation of its content produce the event of the word addressed by God to man. But this event does not have an automatic effect. If the word of God is to be heard as such, the Holy Spirit has to intervene and enlighten the mind of the person reading Holy Scripture or hearing the preaching of the Church. The text of Scripture or the preacher's human words must be brought to life by the Holy Spirit, if they are to become the word of God for the reader or the listener. God then feeds mind and heart with his living word and effects our sanctification.

God is objectively present in his word contained in Scripture and in the biblical preaching of the Church, but the action of the Holy Spirit is needed to enlighten mind and heart so that it may become the living word of God for readers and listeners. There must also be instruction of mind and heart before the speech of God in the Bible can be understood. The objective event of the word of God therefore, requires intermediary human means to reach mind and heart and bring true understanding of biblical language. It demands preachers trained in exegesis to interpret the Scriptures and believers catechised in the rudiments of the faith.

God is objectively present in the Sacraments of his presence and his work — actions of the Church which were instituted by Christ but which require the action of the Holy Spirit for the work of God represented in the sacrament to bear fruit in the person receiving it ; and yet, the sacrament directly affects the recipient without intermediary human means. Here we touch on the difference between word and sacrament. The word of God is addressed to minds and hearts which have to be instructed if they are to understand, so that it really becomes the word of God for the listener. The sacraments affect the person directly, accomplishing objectively what is signified, without the mediation of mind and heart ; although the work of the Holy Spirit acting upon faith is required, if the fruits of the action which the sacraments signify and accomplish, are to be produced. Anyone who is baptised, is placed totally within the benefits of the redemption accomplished by Christ, even if he does not understand what is happening to him — the Church baptises infants — but it is only through the Holy Spirit's gift of faith, that he will be able to bear in his life the fruits of his baptism. Anyone who receives Christ, really present in the Lord's Supper (the Eucharist), receives him completely whatever the state of his faith or his understanding of the mystery effected in him ; but it is only when the Holy Spirit quickens his faith that he can bear in his life the fruit of his communion with Christ, really and objectively present in the Eucharist. The sacrament is the sure sign that God works in us, whatever the state of our belief, our faithfulness or our obedience, in order to show us the power of that love which covers the multitude of our sins ; if we are faithless, he remains faithful, for he cannot deny himself. God is always faithful to the promise he expresses in each sacrament, and he fulfills it in us. Even if we are faithless he cannot deny his promise. But the faithfulness of God in the sacrament constrains us to be faithful in our turn and produce the fruits of the work of God in us, thanks to faith quickened by the Holy Spirit.

The sacrament is a concrete or material sign, instituted by Christ and practised by the apostles and the Church after them, which involves the presence and the action of God. God, present in the sacramental act, accomplishes the spiritual action signified materially by the sacrament. The objective accomplishment of what the sacrament signifies, depends only on the promise of God which is inherent in it, in so far as the Church celebrates it according to the Lord's will. The spiritual fruit of the sacrament, the normal consequences of its objective effect, develops in so far as faith quickened by the Holy Spirit and the word of God, admits the full significance of the sacrament and consents to the movement which it effects in the individual person.

The Church's tradition recognises in the Gospel two major sacraments instituted by Christ — baptism and the Eucharist. However, tradition has retained other signs which some Churches recognise as also being sacraments, instituted by the Lord and practised by the apostles : confirmation, confession, the anointing of the sick, marriage and ordination. Those who recognise only two sacraments, properly speaking, must admit that in the five sacramental acts we have just mentioned,, there are actions and elements, meaning and content which relate them to the two major sacraments of baptism and the Eucharist.

23

BAPTISM

Baptism is the visible sign and the efficacious sacrament of the total remission of sin. Man is born in the state of sin which separates him from God. But Christ lived, died and rose again to reconcile man with God. Through baptism God applies to each one the total forgiveness which Christ won for us in his liberating death. By the baptism of water, man, who was separated from God, is restored to communion with him. Baptism is a plunge into the love of Christ which purifies from all sin. It involves passing with Christ through a spiritual death and burial of sinful man, who is separated from God, for a resurrection into a new life, and the gift of the Holy Spirit, who sanctifies that life. Through baptism, sin is drowned. Sinful man dies. He is buried with Christ and rises with him to a life of faith.

Baptism constitutes our first step towards sharing the life of the Body of Christ, and it has to be taken anew every day. By faith we have continually to take a fresh plunge into the life, death and resurrection of Christ. Baptism by water is the first sign of this rhythm of the Christian life [14].

The baptism of water is a *death* and a *resurrection*. It is the liturgical action by which the

Church brings a person through the mystery of the death and the resurrection of the Lord. In intimate union with Christ, the baptised is, as it were, buried, so that the power of sin may die in him, and he returns to the life which the power of the resurrection of the Son of God awakens in him. The baptism of water is therefore a *purification*. In bringing the baptised through his death, Christ gives him a purifying power which, working together with faith, will always dispose him to receive the Word of God once more. The pouring of water is the efficacious sign of this purification. The baptism of water is a new *birth*, launching the Christian life into the power given by the resurrection of Christ. The primitive symbol of immersion in water signifies death, burial, resurrection and new birth in concrete terms. Baptism by water is *incorporation* into Christ and into the Church. The baptised person who shares in the death and resurrection of Christ becomes one body with him. He is a member of the Body of Christ, the Church. The presence of the Church through the community gathered together for the baptism signifies this incorporation.

The baptism of water is linked with baptism of the Spirit. By the laying on of hands, the Church signifies the gift of the Holy Spirit which comes and dwells in the baptised. Baptism of the Spirit is an *illumination*. The baptised person receives the Holy Spirit who will enlighten him in the faith and allow him to understand the Word of God. The baptism of the Spirit is a *consecration*. The Holy Spirit associates the person baptised in the royal and prophetic priesthood of Christ and of the Church in the world. The baptism of Spirit is a *seal*. The Holy Spirit marks the person baptised so that he may be kept till the last day and recognised as worthy of the Kingdom.

The baptism of water and of Spirit leads to the

Eucharist. When the baptised is able to discern the Lord's Body, he can join in Holy Communion. Catechism prepares the one baptised for this discernment and makes explicit the confession of faith made in baptism. Confirmation is a consecration of baptised members to be available for service in the Church.

The royal and prophetic priesthood of the people of God, to which by baptism in the Spirit the Christian is consecrated has been described by St. Peter : "Come, and let yourselves be built like living stones into the spiritual temple where you will serve as holy priests to offer acceptable spiritual sacrifices to God through Jesus Christ... But you are the chosen race, the King's priests, the holy nation, God's own people, chosen to proclaim the triumphs of God who called you from darkness into his own marvellous light. At one time you were not a people of any sort, but now, you are the Pepole of God ; at one time you knew nothing of God's mercy, but now, you have experienced it for yourselves. I appeal to you, my friends, as exiles and aliens in this world, do not give way to your physical passions which are always fighting against the soul. Let all your behaviour be such as even pagans can recognise as good, and then, although they now malign you as criminals, they will come to see for themselves that you lead good lives, and give glory to God on the Day of his Coming" (1 Pet. 2. 5, 9-12).

Baptism in the Spirit is anointing (christian means anointed). The baptised person is, like Christ, the Anointed of the Lord, prophet, priest and king. He shares in the prophetic, priestly and royal ministry of Christ. He shares in the prophetic ministry of Christ by proclaiming the praises of him who called him out of darkness into his marvellous light. He shares in the priestly ministry of Christ by offering spiritual sacrifices acceptable to God, through Jesus Christ ; he shares in the kingly ministry of Christ by his good life among men so that they may glorify God, on the Day of his Visitation. So, a baptised person is consecrated by the Holy Spirit to bear witness — by his words, by his praise and intercession, and by the goodness of his life — all this for the world and in the world. The baptised fulfils this royal and prophetic priesthood for men so that one day they may glorify God. The sanctification of the baptised is not for his sake alone, but for others, by the shining example of word, prayer and life.

The royal and prophetic priesthood of the baptised does not confer the right to exercise every office in the Church. Sometimes this vague idea of the universal priesthood has been held. The royal and prophetic priesthood is the priesthood of the whole Church, shared by every baptised person for the sake of all, by their prophetic witness in the world, by their priestly prayer for everyone, by the royalty of lives, liberated and luminous, in the midst of men. The royal and prophetic priesthood cannot be confused with the pastoral ministry in the Church which implies a special vocation, special training and a specific ordination.

This priesthood of the laity, the priesthood of the whole Church as the Body of Christ in the world, carries unique dignity and importance. St. Peter shows in the passage quoted above, how this priesthood is fulfilled in the world, in civil and social life, in marriage, in suffering and in persecution (1 Peter 2. 13 to 3. 17). The title of "lay" should always retain its beauty and nobility. It means that a baptised person belongs to the *laos*, the people of God, a holy people, acquired by God to be his own, radiating the glory of the Risen Christ among men.

24

THE EUCHARIST

The Eucharist is the visible sign and efficacious sacrament of the real presence and sanctifying work of Christ in his Church ; he feeds the members of his Body with his very self, really present.

The profound reason for our faith in the real, living presence of Jesus Christ in the Eucharist is that on the evening of Holy Thursday he himself left us this sacrament of his presence, when he said : "This is my body... this is my blood."

The real presence of Christ in the Eucharist is the presence of Christ crucified, risen and glorified, continuing his redeeming work in and through his Church. The real presence is not a static, motionless presence like that of an object, but the living presence of Jesus Christ, making actual for us the redeeming mystery, his unique sacrifice on the cross. That is why we cannot speak of the real presence without first speaking of the presence of the sacrifice of Christ in the Eucharist. The real presence is the presence of Christ crucified and glorious, acting in his Church through the ever-present power of his sacrifice [15].

The primitive Church, faithful to the New Testament, saw in the Eucharist the new paschal meal of the new Covenant. Just as the Jews made present and actual in the annual Passover meal the deliverance of the people of God, accomplished once and for all by the exodus from Egypt, Christians make present and actual in the eucharistic meal the redemption of the people of God, accomplished once and for all on the Cross. In this mystery, we should see a memorial in the biblical sence of the word, that is to say a liturgical action, by which we bless God for all his wonders and remind him of what he has done in the past, of his mercy and his blessings, so that today he may again give a new sign of his love. In this sense the Eucharist, the sacrament or actuality of Christ's sacrifice, is a sacrifice of intercession which implores the grace of the Lord.

The Eucharist is a sacrifice of thanksgiving and a sacrifice of intercession : it is the sacramental *presence* of the sacrifice of the Cross by the power of the Holy Spirit and the Word, and the liturgical *presentation* of this sacrifice of the Son by the Church to the Father, in thanksgiving for all his blessings and in intercession that he may grant them anew ; it is the *participation* of the Church in the intercession of the Son to the Father in the Holy Spirit that all may receive salvation and that the Kingdom may come in glory ; it is the Church's *offering* of herself to the Father, in union with the sacrifice and the intercession of the Son, as her supreme adoration and perfect consecration in the Holy Spirit.

Without detracting in any way from the uniqueness of the Cross, the expiation, the reconciliation and the redemption, the Eucharist is the sacrament or presence of the unique sacrifice, continuing today in the Church the application of salvation, communion with God and the intercession of Christ. The Eucharist is the Cross present in the Church, extending to all mankind in space and time, and in depth, the unique and perfect work of Christ. In the Eucharist the Church meets Christ who gives salvation to each individual, deepens the communion of humanity with God, intercedes for all and hastens the coming of the Kingdom.

The Church has understood the words of Christ : "This is my body... this is my blood..." in a very simple sense, realistic and sacramental at the same time ; realistic, for Christ spoke the truth, and he is really and actually present in the Eucharist ; sacramental, for his presence is not in the flesh as ours is. In the Eucharist the glorified Christ is present for the Church in his whole person, but sacramentally, in a way that is a mystery. For the Church Fathers, the bread and the wine are changed into the body and blood of Christ according to the mystery of God, who takes ordinary bread and wine, and makes them the body and blood of Christ, the sacramental signs of his real presence.

Today, desiring to be faithful, and viewing the question ecumenically, we can sum up our belief in the real presence of Christ in the Eucharist in this way :

a) The body and blood of Christ, all his humanity and all his divinity, are really present in the Eucharist.

This real presence of his body and his blood is the presence of Christ crucified and glorified, here and now in material signs. The meaning of any corporal presence lies in the proof it offers that a person is really present and able to enter into real communication. By the real presence of the body and blood of Christ, the Church is certain that her Lord is there, in the midst, truly and really, and she receives him in that kind, truly and really.

b) By the Holy Spirit and by his Word, Christ takes sovereign mastery of the elements of bread and wine, draws them to himself and takes them up into the fullness of his humanity and his divinity, so that they really become his body and his blood, according to the Gospel.

The glorified Christ takes the form of bread and wine to reveal his corporal presence in the Church. The bread and wine of the Eucharist are no longer ordinary bread and wine. Their chemical nature, certainly, still remains that of bread and of wine, but behind this chemical nature the true and new substantial reality of this bread and wine must be recognised by faith : the body and the blood of Christ. The Church believes that this bread and wine are the body and blood of Christ, in the sense that the glorified Christ takes them and makes of them a material token of his presence in the midst of us (his eucharistic token), where he may be found, contemplated and communicated.

c) The body and the blood of Christ, objectively present in the Eucharist for communion, really and truly affect all who receive them.

St. Paul expresses the objectivity of the eucharistic presence of Christ, by showing the fateful consequences of unbelieving or selfish communion, which discerns neither the body of Christ nor the body of the Church by faith and charity (1 Cor. 11. 27-34). In the case of an unworthy communion, a person without faith and charity encounters Christ, really present, but does not receive the fruits of this encounter. Still, we must remember that the Eucharist is for the poor and the sick, which means all of us, in the weakness of our faith.

d) Communion in the body and blood of Christ is at the same time a communion of each individual in the body of the whole Church. United in one and the same offering in Christ by the Church, the faithful are joined indissolubly together by communion in the body of Christ.

The Church makes the Eucharist, but the Eucharist makes the Church. The Eucharist unites and welds together the members of the body of Christ. United in the body of Christ, eucharistic and ecclesial, all the baptised are bonded together in unity and can only seek to deepen, extend and complete their unity. The Eucharist, sacrament of unity, is also the sacrament of that loving charity which it nourishes and deepens. In the life of a local community, it is supremely by the Eucharist that the Church is built, shaped and deepened in love. The Church which celebrates the Eucharist frequently sees Christ developing her charity and her unity by means of the Eucharist, and making effective her word and her life in the world.

So, all separated Christians can have no greater desire for unity than to be gathered one day in a single faith, in a single eucharistic communion, and that will be the sign that their visible unity has been fully achieved.

25

CONFIRMATION

Confirmation is the consecration of baptised Christians for their service of Christ in the Church. Baptism in the Holy Spirit confers on the Christian a royal priesthood — witnessing in the world, praying for all men and being a light of life. Confirmation is a fresh realisation of this royal priesthood and a consecration of the baptised for service in the Church [16].

Baptism in the Spirit includes the laying on of hands which confers the gifts of the Holy Spirit. These gifts are made plain in the imagery of anointing (illumination and consecration) and of sealing (marking and setting apart for the Kingdom). Confirmation repeats the act of the laying on of hands which transmits the gifts of the Holy Spirit. It confers the renewal of the Spirit and the gifts necessary for service in the Church; it takes up again the idea of illumination and of consecration, signified by the image of anointing.

This confirmation-consecration is set within the royal priesthood of all baptised in water and in the Spirit. Their first responsibility as lay people is towards the world by their witness, their interceding and their influence; but a Church, which is not inclined to be clerical, also desires to involve them in service to their fellow-Christians, and it is confirmation which consecrates them by the Holy Spirit for this service of the Church.

Confirmation is a strengthening of the Christian in the royal priesthood ; it renews in him the gifts of the Holy Spirit for his warfare in the world, a warfare of witness, intercession and sanctification. It also consecrates him to be available to serve the Church. It is not right, in the anxiety to avoid clericalism, to assign any and every function to the laity. Lay people cannot take on the charge of ordained ministers. The surest way of avoiding the clericalisation of the whole Church is to refrain from turning lay people into ministers of sorts, keeping them rather as much as possible "in the thick of things", in their royal priesthood of prayer for all mankind and witness to the world. Of course, there is a proper collaboration between laity and ministry, which confirmation consecrates. This collaboration cannot be precisely determined in advance ; it will depend on what the Church requires. First and foremost it is a matter of being available for service and being willing to collaborate with the ordained ministers. It is however possible to quote examples of what this lay service of confirmed Christians involves.

In accordance with the threefold ministry, of Christ, the Church and the royal priesthood, confirmed Christians are designated, as lay people, for prophetic, priestly and royal service in the Church.

By way of prophetic service, we may think of the teaching role of the laity. Once they themselves have been taught the faith in the on-going instruction of the Church, confirmed lay Christians may become catechists ; or take responsibility for a group in the parish — a youth group, or a neighbourhood group ; or exercise pastoral care, with their minister.

As for priestly service we may think of the role lay Christians can play in the liturgy. A confirmed Christian may be called to help in the worship of the Church, by reading from the Bible, leading intercessory prayers or taking up the offerings. A lay person may be asked to lead a service.

As for royal service, think of the hospitality ordinary lay people can offer. Hospitality is an important function of the Church. St. Peter, whose description of the royal priesthood of the laity we have already quoted, exhorts "Give hospitality to one another, and ungrudgingly" (1 Pet. 4. 9). In the Epistle to the Hebrews we are reminded of the "mystery" of hospitality. "Persevere in brotherly love ; do not neglect hospitality, for some have entertained angels unawares" (Heb. 13. 1-2). Hospitality, visiting others, being friendly and welcoming — all are a real service each lay person can render, showing love for Christ and for the Church, and preparing an authentic, loving community for those who are discovering their Christian vocations.

26

CONFESSION

The ministry of absolution is part of the mission of the apostles and of the Church. Jesus illustrated and signified this forgiveness by healing a paralysed man. The Church declares the absolution of sins and raises miraculously the person paralysed by his own faults, performing a work of spiritual resurrection. The Risen Lord is working through her. It was the Risen Lord on Easter evening who conferred on his apostles and through them on the Church, the power and the mission of forgiveness. The Lord told them : "Peace be with you ; as the Father sent me, I send you." The Father sent the Son who has power on earth to forgive sins, and the Son similarly sends the Church with this same power. "When he had said that, he breathed on them and said : "Receive the Holy Spirit. If you forgive sins, they are forgiven ; if you retain sins, they are retained" (John 20. 22-23).

The breath of the Spirit has to do with life, healing and resurrection. The Creator's breath created a living being. Elijah's breath restored life to a dying child. Ezekiel invoked the breath of the Spirit to raise up the people of God. It is in this context of healing, resurrection and renewal that we are to understand Christ's gesture ; what he gives to his disciples is a gift of spiritual resurrection. The

Church receives power to revive an individual spiritually by remitting his sins. It is because sin deprives us of the real life which we received on the day of creation and which was renewed in Jesus Christ that we need the very breath of the Holy Spirit to resurrect us. The Church must make use of this gift of the re-creating breath, which Christ transmitted to the apostles.

The gift the apostles received on that first Easter evening should not be identified with the gift of proclaiming the good news. Christ promised, first to St. Peter, and then to all the apostles, that whatever the Church bound on earth would be bound in heaven and all that the Church loosed would be loosed (Matt. 16. 19 ; 18. 18) ; this concerns the whole apostolic ministry. It was for the totality of this ministry that the apostles received the fullness of the Holy Spirit at Pentecost ; but here it is a question of one specific gift. The apostles and the Church proclaim the Gospel and remit sins. They receive a special charisma, promise, mission and ministry. This ministry is one aspect of the power of the keys, which should be applied to all the work of the Church as a whole for the liberation of mankind. That gift, promise, mission and ministry is the power of absolution. Here it is not just a question of the preaching ministry, but really and truly of a word and an act which effectively achieve what they signify. Christ does not say that sins are forgiven when people, by faith, apply to themselves the promise of forgiveness announced in the preaching of the word. He says : "If you forgive sins, they are forgiven." Here we have an example of a sacramental act. There is a sacramental action when, as Jesus Christ promised, the Church believes that God acts conjointly and effectively in a sign given by her to the believer [17].

At this point we must consider the spiritual

value of the sign of absolution added to the simple preaching of forgiveness. Here we touch on the necessary distinction between the announcement of the word of God and the sacramental signs. In the Word, written and preached, the promise of Jesus Christ is proclaimed to us. By faith and prayer, the works of the Holy Spirit in us, we can make this promise become a reality. I can listen to a sermon on the infinite mercy of God and turn forgiveness into an effective reality, if I receive this preaching with a sincere act of faith and a prayerful spirit. But it is possible for me not to understand or not really to hear this message of liberation. I may doubt if it really is addressed to me personally, I may think myself not sufficiently sinful, or on the other hand too sinful. In this sacrament, God in a way forces the faith of the believer, weak though it may be, and makes real in and for him the work signified by the sacrament, far beyond all that he asks or thinks.

In the sign of absolution, the mercy of God is not only offered to faith and prayer as a promise which will be fulfilled ; all whose sins are remitted by the Church, founded on Jesus Christ and the apostles, are actually and personally forgiven. So the sign of absolution effectively confers what it signifies. The word of God which declares the promise of mercy made by Jesus Christ, must be made concrete in the sign of absolution, and the believer must realise that the forgiveness of sins is not only a hope but a present and actual fact to which he can cling with all his faith.

Even those who are well-persuaded of the sound grounds for confession, may stumble over various practical difficulties. First of all the danger of habit which in the long run can reduce the feeling of repentance and the joy of absolution. In this connection we should mention that, just as with the Eucharist, psychological emotions should not be our prime expectation. If absolution has sacramental value, it produces the effect of remission of sins and reconciliation with God, forges once again our friendship with Christ and renews our communion with the whole Church, quite independently of sensations and feelings. Joy and peace are gifts which God may grant us, but they are not essential for a genuine confession. Conviction of sin, sincere repentance and faith in God's mercy are sufficient to make our confession genuine. It is not because a Eucharist or a confession have moved us, that they have more value. Christ is present and sins are forgiven ; our feelings need not necessarily be stirred.

Another difficulty arises from the fact that very often our sin repeats itself and we are obliged to keep on confessing the same things. This is perhaps a sign of inadequate self-examination, when we are blinded by one single aspect of our sinfulness. It is the duty of the spiritual director to draw attention to a sin which has been ignored or passed over in silence ; we may be kept from seeing it by a fault which is perhaps not very serious, but which worries us. It is certain that absolution does not free us from a particular sin from one day to the next. We must remember that the first aim of absolution is not psychological liberation, but spiritual certainty of God's forgiveness. Even if we know that deliverance will not be swift, it is necessary to ask for pardon and to receive in faith the remission of sins. Absolution can be compared to a remedy which must be taken if we are to live, even if we think it will not effect an immediate cure.

The certainty of the mercy of Christ which is nourished by absolution is indispensable to a full spiritual life. A Christian will seek it in order to deepen his inner life, even if he finds he is not rid of a sin which he is obliged to keep on confessing. In sacramental absolution we must recognise a mystery which, by setting a person once more in Christ, gives him an inkling of the world to come. As at the Eucharist, he stands in an eschatological situation. He lives in anticipation the return of Christ and finds himself, during the time of the sacrament, with those inclinations to holiness and purity with which the Lord will fill him on the last day.

The sacramental mystery of confession is like a much-needed bath, which washes us clean, but does not prevent us from becoming soiled once more. Only if we prolong the sacrament in faith and obedience can we be victorious, partially in this world, finally on the day of the coming of our Lord Jesus Christ. This tension between the sacrament, which brings us an inkling of the other world, and daily life, which plunges us into time, leads us to repeat with the first Christians our one great hope : "Maranatha, come Lord ; the Lord is coming."

27

ANNOINTING OF THE SICK

The risen Lord has triumphed over all the powers of evil ; he has full power to heal the sick, for he reigns over our bodies as he reigns over our entire being. While he lived on earth, Christ frequently demonstrated his power to heal the sick. In the Gospels healing always has deep significance. It is a sign of the Saviour's compassion for suffering humanity, and a sign of spiritual resurrection by the forgiveness of sins.

Since God loves us, he wants to relieve our pains and our suffering, but he may also want to maintain us in our sickness. He gives it significance, makes it an effective way of praying for others, and for the sick to grow spiritually too. Healing is never just a miracle ; it is a sign of the love of God and the inner resurrection of man. This inner sense of the sign of healing also exists without any outward sign ; if God judges illness to be more helpful for the sick person and for those around him, he may be unwilling to grant the sign. That is why we can never demand the sign of healing, but only open our selves to receive it, if God so wills.

It is the Church's mission to demonstrate her faith in the victorious power of Christ over the body and over disease ; she should practise a ministry of healing to show that she expects miracles to be always possible. In her ministry, the Church places herself at Christ's disposal and he acts in her and through her. She does not impose her intentions on God, but she performs the actions he has commanded so that his will may be revealed. So the Church performs a ministry for healing, giving the laying-on of hands or anointing the sick, in obedient expectation that the will of God will be fulfilled.

Healing, like every miracle, is a sign that the disorder of fallen creation is challenged as Christ establishes the Kingdom of God, that Kingdom whose glorious appearing is always possible, at any moment. In this sense, healing is an eschatological sign, announcing the imminent manifestation of the Kingdom, where there will be no more pain, no more sighing from sickness and suffering. The Church desires, and rejoices that physical miracles accompany her preaching from time to time ; they give it persuasive support before the incredulous attitude of many. The Church does not consider miracles to be an illusion created by the hunger of the human psyche for the sensational, but sees them as a sign given by God to confirm her words and to strengthen faith.

The Church has inherited the gifts and ministries entrusted to the apostles ; so she has also received the gift and the ministry of healing, like the Twelve, who, as Christ commanded, preached repentance, cast out many evil spirits, anointed many sick people and healed them (Mark 6. 12-13). The Church obeys the words of St. James : "If anyone of you is sick, let him call in the elders of the Church to pray over him after they have anointed him in the name of the Lord ; the prayer of faith will save the man of patience and the Lord will raise him up ; if he has committed sins, they will be forgiven" (James 5. 14-15).

There is a link between sin and sickness ; not between one particular sin and one particular sickness, but between the state of sin in which mankind finds itself, which has brought about its present disorder, and disease, which is one of the manifestations of this disorder. So confession and absolution are part of the ministry of healing by the laying-on of hands and by anointing. Indeed, St. James continues the passage quoted above : "And so confess your sins to one another and pray for one another that you may be healed."

Confession, and the prayers of intercession continuing it, are for healing : healing which should be understood in its fullest sense as a resurrection of our whole being by the Lord. The ministry of healing, confession and intercession demands vigilance and obedience on the part of the Church, her ministers and her members, although its effectiveness does not depend on them. God is faithful ; he heals, forgives and answers prayers, infinitely beyond all that we ask or think ; his working is free, independent of our obedience, but, for all that, he requires of his Church a vigilance and an obedience which will both express and strengthen her faith. Indeed, it is always to faith that God responds, even in the sacrament. Contrary to what is too often supposed, fervour is not some kind of psychic excitement, it is the gift of one's whole self in an act of faith and in intercession. Our whole being should be offered to God in quiet confidence. Fervour can involve undertaking some form of ascetic discipline, for example fasting, to emphasize the earnestness of our prayer. So, when the Church undertakes a ministry of healing, confession and intercession, spiritual disciplines must not be neglected.

Fervent prayer for healing is accompanied by the outward signs of the laying-on of hands and the anointing with oil, following the practice of the apostles. These actions form part of the Church's ministry for the sick. They signify that she is awaiting the visible effects of the gift of healing [18]. The laying-on of hands upon the sick is the sign by which the Church opposes the power of evil. Anointing with oil is the sign by which the Church gives the power of the Holy Spirit to consecrate a sick person for a special ministry of intercession while he is sick, and for the total healing of his whole person.

The Church has to commit herself to believing that the sick are healed; she has to believe in miracles and at the same time be open to the will of God; such fervour and obedience are the fruits of the Church's preaching and of spiritual direction. The consistent effect of the ministry of healing is the renewal in repentance and faith of the member who is sick and of the whole Christian community; every sacramental action of the Church only renews and deepens the fullness given at baptism.

28

MARRIAGE AND CELIBACY

Christian marriage is a union in human love, sanctified by the love called charity, which is a gift of God.

Christian marriage is not a simple contract of faithfulness between two people who love one another and want to set up a home together. It has its source, its foundation and guarantee in God. When two people unite in Christian marriage, they know that they are no longer two, but one in the sight of God. God commits himself with them in their marriage. He makes and consecrates their union. The human commitment of marriage, based on the love of a man and a woman, receives a sacramental dimension from the commitment and consecration of God, who also desires this union, sets it upon the foundation of his love and his faithfulness, and guarantees it against the risks of disagreement and breakdown. "They are no longer two," said Christ, "but one flesh. What God has joined, man must not separate" (Matt. 19. 6). Because of God's involvement and his consecration attested by words of Christ, which correspond to the human act uniting two people, Christian marriage has sacramental value. It is a human contract of faithfulness which includes the faithfulness of God and the consecration of his Spirit. United in God and by God, Christian partners can never separate without contradicting the will of God, who in spite of all human unfaithfulness, remains faithful to his promise and his blessing [19].

Christian marriage is a mystery, a sign of the love uniting Christ and the Church. St. Paul writes : "Husbands, love your wives as Christ loved the Church" (Eph. 5. 25). Then, quoting, as Jesus did, the text from Genesis on which he bases the "mystery" of marriage, he says : "That is why a man will leave his father and his mother to unite with his wife, and the two shall be one flesh. This mystery has great implications. I mean that it applies to Christ and the Church..." (Eph. 5. 31-32). If the apostle can exhort man and woman in this way to conform to the relationship uniting Christ and the Church, it is because at the creation (Gen. 2. 24), in the institution of marriage itself, there is a great mystery. So Christian marriage is a symbol of the unity of Christ and the Church in the generous and self-sacrificing love of charity. This is the second aspect of the sacramental character of marriage. In their life together Christians have therefore to strive to exemplify in practice the symbol constituted by their union. They have to sacrifice themselves for one another, generously, following the example of Christ and the Church. They are a living proclamation of the mystery of the mutual love of the Church and Christ.

Christian marriage is consecrated and blessed by a liturgical act of the Church. The Holy Spirit is invoked upon the Christian couple, that their union may be consecrated, and that they may have the strength to live out in their life together what they really are — united in God and a symbol of the mutual love of the Church and Christ. That is the third aspect of the sacramental character of Christian marriage. Not only does God commit himself to their union which he founds and guarantees, not only are they the symbol of the union of Christ and the Church, but they also receive the Holy Spirit who sanctifies their union. So, physical human love receives a dignity which makes it a symbol of the generous and self-sacrificing love of Christian charity. Husband and wife no longer belong to themselves but to one another, each giving and sacrificing everything to the other. This becomes possible in the Holy Spirit who consecrates the marriage for ever. "The gifts and the calling of God are irrevocable" (Rom. 11. 29). The Holy Spirit who fills Christian couples with his gifts and calls them to faithfulness, makes of their marriage an indissoluble union.

Christian marriage founds the Christian family. Christian couples welcome with joy the children God grants them. Their union is not just for themselves — egoistic and withdrawn ; it is at the service of Christ and of the Church, which is why they desire a family who will glorify God in love, joy and freedom. Their commitment with regard to their children, given them as visible signs of their love, is the fourth aspect of the sacramental character of marriage. Children, gifts of God, are a new consecration of the marriage. They renew the bond of union. They deepen the faithfulness of the partners in their love for one another, in their endeavour to transmit life, joy and liberty.

The way of Christian marriage is not easy. It presupposes a vocation, a choice, a commitment, sacrifices and difficulties. To the apostles, who were astonished at the demands of marriage formulated by Christ, he replied : "Not everyone can understand, only those who have been given understanding" (Mat. 19. 11).

All Christians are not called to marry. Some receive the vocation to remain in celibacy for the sake of Christ and the Kingdom of God. Normally these Christians are called to live in community for a special service of God and the Church, in liturgical praise, a common life and the gift of themselves to their neighbours. Christian celibacy has three main meanings : diaconal — it sets a person free for Christ's service ; contemplative — it favours the life of prayer ; eschatological — it heralds the Kingdom of God [20].

Christian celibacy allows a freedom and an availability in life and ministry which make it very appropriate to the service of the Church. Voluntary celibacy for the sake of the Kingdom of Heaven establishes not only a spiritual but also a real resemblance to Christ. Following the example of Christ, the Christian celibate can devote himself entirely to ministry. All his preoccupations can be focused on work for God. All his powers can be centred on a living proclamation of the Gospel to hasten the return of Christ. He is ready and able to respond to calls from the Church and his community.

Anyone who knows the solitude of voluntary celibacy can only desire to live for Christ alone depending on him, and on his friendship. The Christian celibate seeks to please his Lord in a life of contemplation. The liturgical life of a monastic community bears a direct relationship to this intention of pleasing the Lord. Liturgical and contemplative prayer constantly place the monk beside Christ in the attitude of John the Baptist, who declared : "It is the bridegroom who has the bride, but the bridegroom's friend, standing beside him listening, thrills with joy when the bridegroom speaks. That is my joy and now it is perfect" (John 3. 29). Christ has had no other bride than the Church, and the disciple of Christ has no greater friend than the Bridegroom of the Church. It is enough for him to stand beside the Bridegroom and hear him. The Bridegroom's voice rejoices his heart in prayer and contemplation. This dependence is perfection of joy for the celibate disciple.

Celibacy is a sign of the Resurrection and the coming Kingdom of God. At the Resurrection and in the Kingdom there is neither marrying, nor giving in marriage. In the Kingdom of God there will be such fullness of love that we shall no longer feel the need of a limited intimacy. On the contrary, there it would seem like a lessening of love. So Christian celibates are signs of that fullness of love which will be realised in the Kingdom.

Commitment to voluntary celibacy, together with community of goods and obedience to a rule and an authority, is part of the monastic vocation, this, like marriage, is permanent in character. It is an indissoluble bond of faithfulness to Christ and to the community one has entered to serve. In the act of monastic commitment, God commits himself both by the call which he gives and by the gifts which he grants. Christ has promised to all wo give up everything for him and for the Gospel, in particular the prospect of marriage and family life, a hundred times more at present, and in the world to come everlasting life. So the monk must believe that this irrevocable promise is being fulfilled for him, once he has definitively committed himself so to live for Christ (Luke 18. 29-30). God does not go back on his gifts, nor his call (Rom. 11. 29). In this certainty the Christian monk finds peace and the availability necessary for effective prayer and ministry. God is faithful and never repents of the call he has addressed to us, nor of his gifts ; this assurance kindles joy in our hearts, stifling any secret groaning under the burden of a ministry or a state we sometimes might wish otherwise.

Some Christians are called to accept or to desire celibacy for the love and the service of Christ, without a vocation for the monastic life. Seeing the difficulty of living in such solitude out in the world, they will seek to establish bonds of fellowship with others who share the same vocation. Celibacy may not necessarily imply life in a monastic community, it does nonetheless require a strong bond of fellowship to support the inner commitment.

29

ORDINATION TO THE MINISTRY

The apostles instituted ministries, given by the Spirit, through the laying on of hands, to proclaim the gospel, celebrate the sacraments and gather the Christian community together for its mission. They transmitted their authority, as guardians of the faith entrusted to them, and as responsible for its faithful transmission, to "dependable men", successors of the apostles and supervisors of the Church. The laying-on of hands, performed in submission to the Holy Spirit, with discernment and in order, so as to keep providing the Church with ministers as signs of the ministry of Christ, is an objective feature of the apostolic tradition.

Through ordination, the Holy Spirit is granted to people who become instruments of Christ building up his Church into a priestly kingdom, a prophetic body in the world. As instruments, the ordained ministers give their lives to Christ, offering their minds and their hearts their words and their gestures, so that Christ as prophet, apostle and teacher can proclaim his word ; so that Christ, as priest and intercessor, can celebrate the sacraments and pronounce praise and intercessions ; so that Christ, king, bishop and pastor can lead his people in unity and obedience, until his Kingdom comes. The laying-on of hands is part of the sacred deposit which must be preserved, since it continually produces the necessary signs and instruments of the pastorate of Jesus Christ in his Church, so that she may become a kingdom of prophets and priests, that God may so be glorified, and the world believe.

The ordination of the ministers of the Church is an apostolic institution, an integral part of the sacred deposit of the faith, since it endows the Church with signs and instruments of the ministry of Christ in the word and the sacraments. Without ordination, the Church could not be certain that the ministers she institutes into a charge, after vocation and training, are truly vested with the power of the Holy Spirit for their ministry, truly fit to transmit the word of God and celebrate Christ's sacraments, in the truth of the Spirit — she could not be certain that they are in truth authentic agents of the tradition of the Gospel in the Church. Certainly God is free, and the Spirit blows where it will. Christ proclaims his word and reveals his presence through prophets, witnesses and faithful lives ; whenever two or three meet in his name, he is among them. He is not bound exclusively by the ordination of ministers. But ordination is indispensable to transmit the Holy Spirit which unites the apostles with their successors and their collaborators as true guardians of the sacred deposit of the faith.

The laying-on of hands could be given by a presbyter acting as a collective bishop : "Do not neglect the gift of the Spirit (the charisma) which is in you. It was given to you when the prophets spoke and the elders as a body laid their hands upon you" (1 Tim. 4. 14). It could also be given by the apostle himself : "I remind you to stir into flame the gift of the Spirit of God (the charisma of God) which is within you through the laying-on of my hands" (2 Tim. 1. 6). It can be given by the succesor of an apostle (1 Tim. 5. 22). But it is always the apostolic college acting in the name of Christ, to join to itself successors or collaborators by the laying-on of hands which confers the Holy Spirit, for the faithful transmission of the Gospel in the Church, through the word of God and the sacraments of his presence. The Spirit is given through the laying-on of hands by the apostles (Acts 8. 18). They are ever present to the Church and it is they who always continue to ensure an unbroken succession of ministry for the faithful safekeeping of the sacred deposit of the faith and the authentic tradition of the gospel. That is what the Church was later to signify, by attributing the ministry of ordination to bishops alone, as signs of the presence of the apostles in the Church for her government. However, the idea of a collective episcopate exercised by a college of presbyters, having the ministry of ordination, is neither foreign nor contrary to the practice of the early Church, in certain regions [21]. What is important is that the bishop, be he individual or collective, should intend to act in succession to the apostles and in communion with them, to confer on new ministers the gift of the Holy Spirit, so as to institute them to be signs and instruments of the pastorate of Jesus Christ in his Body the Church. The minister of the ordination is the apostle who is always present in the Church through the intermediary of his successor, the bishop, individual or collegial. Most frequently the Church unites two traditions, recognising the minister of ordination in the bishop, as the successor of the apostles, acting in and with the college of presbyters, collaborators with the apostles.

There is but one good pastor or shepherd, the Lord Jesus. He leads his people, the Church, with perfect wisdom and safety. He knows each of those who belong to him and desires to lead them all into his Kingdom without losing a single one. Christ, the great pastor, bishop or guardian of our lives, is, as his title indicates, the one on whom the Father bestowed the perfect anointing (charisma), the one on whom he set his seal at his baptism in the Jordan. Now, under the old Covenant, those who received anointing were the prophets, the priests and the kings. Christ received anointing as prophet, priest and king ; he possesses the fullness of the power of God over his people, he is the perfect and final successor of Moses, Aaron and David.

Christ is prophet ; he has given us the word of God contained in the Gospel ; by the Holy Spirit he leads us into the whole truth. Christ is priest ; he died for us on the cross, offering to the Father the perfect sacrifice and the effective intercession which was to save us for ever and always ; he offers eternally in heaven what he did once and for all, and his presence with the Father is a living inter-cession on our behalf. Christ is King ; he is risen, he is enthroned Lord of the Church and of the world ; by his power he directs all things, in unity with the Father and the Holy Spirit.

Christ has formed the faithful into his Church : she is his Body and his Spouse, his instrument and also his fellow-worker for his continuing work on earth until he returns. It was the will of Christ that the Church should share in his threefold ministry to continue his acts : the Church is a royal and prophetic priesthood. The Church is a prophetic community with the task of proclaiming the praises of him who has called us out of darkness into his marvellous light : the Church has a ministry of preaching and of teaching which she performs in her worship, her catechising and her theology. The Church is a holy priesthood, called to offer spiritual sacrifices, pleasing to God, through Jesus Christ : the Church has a ministry of praise and intercession which she performs in her liturgy. The Church is a royal people, conducting herself so well among the nations that they may be brought to glorify God on

the day of his Coming : the Church has a ministry
of shining example ; she does not preach lessons of
morality to the world, rather she demonstrates by
her life the power of the Risen Christ who alone
procures peace.

Giving and establishing ordained ministries, the
Lord organises the royal and prophetic priesthood
of the Church in the world, exercised by all the
faithful together. The pastoral ministry in the
Church is essentially a ministry of the word, of
sacraments and of unity ; it is the visible sign of the
love of Christ for the Church : he feeds her with
his Word and with his Body, he leads her to the
eternal Kingdom.

The specific character of the pastor's charge is
to be the servant of a community where all are
brothers together. He feeds them with the word and
the sacraments ; he leads them in the way of unity.
The bishop is the pastor of a local or regional Church,
in a city or in a region embracing several communities ; he represents the unity of the communities
among themselves and their unity with the other
Churches in the universal Church [22].

The pastor is the minister of Christ as prophet :
he preaches and teaches the word of God. The pastor
is the minister of Christ as priest : he celebrates
the Eucharist, recalling before the Father the unique
and perfect sacrifice of Christ ; he intercedes for the
sanctification of the whole Church and of each one
of the faithful. The pastor is the minister of Christ
the king : he incorporates new members into the
Body of Christ by baptism, associating them in the
royal and prophetic priesthood ; he consecrates
servants of the Church by confirmation ; he fights
against sin and evil by giving absolution and by the
laying of hands on the sick, he blesses marriage, and
every human situation, for its sanctification ; he

shares the gifts of the Spirit which he has received, by laying his hands on new pastors, with his colleagues, under the presidence of the bishop representing the unity of the Church ; as the minister of Christ the King, the pastor also exercises authority as the servant who gathers the Christian community together for her mission.

The laying-on of hands at ordination is the effective sign of the gifts of the Holy Spirit granted to the minister for his ministry ; God involves himself in this gesture of the Church and gives what he has promised : the power of his Spirit. The laying-on of hands is a sacramental act which produces what it stands for.

Ordination has a definitive character — the minister of the Church commits himself to be a pastor until the return of Christ, which he is called to prepare. Only synodical or ecumenical authority could relieve him of his charge for some important reason.

The ordained ministry is compatible with an employment, which may even be necessary in certain situations, in order to make better contact with people. The ordained ministry may cease to be exercised for a time, but a new ordination is not required when it is resumed.

The ordained ministry of word, sacraments and unity may be exercised in a great diversity of forms of ministry according to the Church's needs.

If the unity of a Christian community demands a pastoral ministry, if the unity of the communities in a given region demands a pastoral ministry, if the unity of the communities in a given region demands an episcopal ministry, does the unity of regional Churches in the universal Church likewise demand a particular ministry ? Tradition has recognised the value of the ministry of patriarchs who group under their authority a certain number of regional Churches. But do these patriarchs themselves have to recognise the primacy of one of their number ? The Bishop of Rome has seen his ministry gradually extend to the role of primate and arbiter in the universal Church. This authority is not recognised as his by all the Churches. But at a time when the visible unity of Christians is being reconstituted, is it not necessary to re-think the universal ministry of the Bishop of Rome in relation to all the Churches ? Between the meetings of ecumenical Councils, it is useful that a universal authority should be at the service of the unity of all the Churches in faith and in charity. It is true that the meetings of a universal synod representing all the Churches can ensure this ministry of unity. But such a synod has to be presided over, ordered and continued in the intervals between sessions. Could not the Bishop of Rome, recognised by tradition as filling this universal function, be accepted by all the Churches as the servant of the servants of God ? If the tradition of the universal Church has more authority than that of a local Church or than the faith of one individual Christian, does it not need one voice to express it ? The Bishop of Rome might find again, in the unity of all the Churches, a ministry as servant of the universal faith expressed by the Councils and a ministry of arbitration in the conflicts which might endanger visible unity.

30

PRAYER

Our response to the gifts God abundantly pours upon us by his grace, in his word and his sacraments, is prayer, the liturgical prayer of the Church and the personal prayer of the Christian. But it is the Holy Spirit within us who gives our hearts the desire to pray, for we can do nothing in the spiritual life without the constant help of the grace of God.

The Holy Spirit is the Counsellor who prays with us and in us, as St. Paul asserts : "The Spirit comes to the help of our weakness, for we do not know how we ought to pray ; but the Spirit himself pleads for us in sighs too deep for words. He who sounds the depths of our hearts, knows what the Spirit means and that his intercession for God's people corresponds to the will of God" (Rom. 8. 26-27). So it is God who is the source and end of our praying. He gives the desire to pray and he inspires its intentions through the Holy Spirit, who comes to strengthen our weakness in spiritual living ; he intercedes for us ; and he unites us with Christ, our intercessor with the Father, in one single prayer.

The Father wants to bring us into intimacy and cooperation with him through prayer. Prayer is the Father's will as the way for us to converse and work with him. Not only witness and ministry, but also praying makes us fellow-workers with God. It is this dialogue and this work shared with the Father which are the fundamental reasons for prayer ; so we are united to the life of God.

Christians pray in the name of Christ, our Lord. By prayer we are united with the Son in his work of intercession to the Father. Prayer establishes us in a very special relationship of communion with the Son.

Thus, the life of prayer brings us into the relationship of Father, Son and Holy Spirit. In our weakness we call on the Holy Spirit who comes to help us in the spiritual life, praying with us and in us, and so uniting us with the Son who intercedes with the Father. The Son presents to the Father the supplications and praise of all the faithful, and of all the saints, in his whole Body, the Church ; he unites them with his own intercession in which he presents his unique sacrifice to the Father, as a perpetual memorial, an invocation, so that all the supplications of men may be granted in his name. The Father grants the Son's intention, as he gathers together all our prayers offered in his name, inspired as they are by the Holy Spirit.

Christian prayer is certain to be answered, not necessarily exactly as it was intended or desired, but within the plan and according to the will of the Father. All the answers to our prayers have to fit into the general pattern of the salvation and well-being of mankind, our own and that of our neighbour as well. All the answers to our prayers set us more firmly in the communion and the love of Christ, our joy and happiness in him. "Ask and you will receive, so that your joy may be full" (John 16. 24).

The Father answers us in the name of Christ, because of his perfect obedience, his unique sacrifice and his effective intercession ; he also answers us in the Church. We do not pray alone, nor are we the only ones to be answered. All the prayers of the faithful are gathered up in the prayer of the Church and brought by the Son before the Father. Likewise, all the answers must be brought into harmony with the universal working of God and contribute to the salvation and happiness of all.

The prayer of the Church as a local and the universal community is the liturgy, the action of the people of God at prayer.

In the liturgy the Church is united with Christ, her intercessor with the Father ; it is Christ himself acting in her who brings her to praise and prayer. He it is who acts through his ministers to proclaim his word and to manifest his presence and grace in the sacraments.

The liturgy is also the prayer of the whole Christian community. The individual has to efface himself to allow the praise and prayer of the Christian community and of the whole Church to be expressed through him. This attitude of ecclesial communion does not mean that the individual is passive. The objectivity and universality of the liturgy do not dispense the believer from participating wholeheartedly.

The liturgy also unites all the Church on earth with all the cloud of witnesses who are now in peace. So, the liturgy is an echo on earth of the praise of the angels and saints, invisibly present with Christ in the assembled community.

The liturgy which is life, commitment and a reflection of the incarnation, involves the whole being of man and all creation. The various sacraments and symbols of the liturgy show the unity in Christ of the two orders, the order of creation and the order of redemption ; they signify that the life of the Christian forms one whole, that it is not divided into a personal social life to be sanctified, and an inner spiritual life which sanctifies. The life of the liturgy overflows into the Christian's entire life, shaping it, stimulating it and giving it its fullest meaning.

The liturgy is the festival of the family of God, where each one can find the expression of his praise and his prayers, his joy and his comfort. It is the place of peace in God, where our energies are restored to confront the world. But it is also the place where we exercise in God's presence our Christian function of service to others. In the liturgy we offer the sacrifice of our lives in union with the perfect sacrifice of Christ ; in this act of offering ourselves and the world to the Father through Christ and the Holy Spirit, we are continually learning to give ourselves in our daily lives for the love of humankind.

The Life

31

LIFE IN CHRIST

Christian life is lived in communion with Christ, through the presence of the Holy Spirit, for the glory of the Father. The Christian life finds its source in the truth perceived by faith. It is nourished by the means of grace, the word and the sacraments, and by prayer, both personal and liturgical. It is lived out in human everyday life in the family, in the community and in society.

The Christian's whole life is summed up in the expression "life in Christ". The Christian life does not consist in observing laws ; it is entirely a matter of striving to be conformed to Christ, a striving prompted by the Holy Spirit who sanctifies each Christian.

"To live, is Christ" (Phil. 1. 21). Since Christ has revealed what it is to be truly man, it is in communion with the humanity of Jesus Christ that the Christian discovers what his human life is meant to be. So St. Paul can offer us this invitation : "Have the same attitude to one another that Christ had : ... Living the life of a man, he humbled himself still more, and was obedient to death, death on a cross" (Phil. 2. 5).

This life does not consist in an outward imitation of Christ, which would be impossible for us, but in a communion with him, in which we let him fill our being completely ; so that he may live in us and conform us to his life. St. Paul also says : "I am crucified with Christ. My life here and now is not my life, but the life Christ lives in me. I live my present life in this body by faith in the Son of God who loved me and gave his life for me" (Gal. 2. 19-20). The Christian's life consists then in dying to self, in crucifying the individual, self-centred 'I', so that Christ can take possession of his whole being and live in the person he transfigures by his presence. The Christian continues to live in the body : he remains fully human and himself ; but the life of faith binds him so closely to the Son of God, conforms him so completely to his love and to his sacrifice, that he is, so to speak, taken out of himself and able to say : "It is no longer I, but Christ, who is living in me."

Faith, awakened in our hearts by the Holy Spirit, binds us to God, giving us full confidence in his guidance and assuring us of the truth of his revelation. Faith dominates the Christian's entire life, because of his affection for God and the confidence and assurance faith creates. Abraham is called the father of the faithful, for by his life and his obedience he gave all men the example of a life inspired by faith. At God's call, he left his country, not knowing where he was going ; when he was commanded to sacrifice his son, the heir to the promise, he obeyed, not knowing how God would pursue his plan ; but the Lord stopped him and gave him back his son.

So life for the Christian is a life in faith. The Christian must live in the certainty that God desires his joy and well-being, and nothing else. This life in faith also implies a spirit of poverty which means that he expects everything from God alone. The Christian knows that by himself he can do nothing ; so he expects everything from God's grace, and this expectancy is an attitude of faith. This spirit of poverty allows him not to fear but actually love a state of material poverty, in which, more than in prosperity, he learns to expect everything from God alone. This attitude of faith means that the Christian can rejoice even when he feels weak and poverty-stricken, for then the power of God reveals itself in him. Human strength and success could form a barrier to the power of God. In our weakness, on the contrary, all the strength we have comes from God. "It is when I am weak, says St. Paul, that I am strong" (2 Cor. 12. 10).

Hope, which is the fruit of faith, gives the Christian an invincible optimism. In the first place hope is directed to the fulfilment of God's promises. The Christian lives hoping for the glorious return of Christ and he expects him every day, he hopes in the resurrection when he will see once more all whom he loved on earth, and he hopes in the life eternal of the Kingdom of God, a life of joy, of peace, of love and praise.

But hope also applies to the immediate future of his life on earth. The Christian knows that God always keep his promises and that he wills to achieve the well-being of all. The Christian always hopes that the next moment will be the happy fulfilment of the present, and that tomorrow will be better than today ; so he advances from hope to hope. St. Paul says that love hopes everything. If the Christian is really possessed by love, love for God and love for people, he can never despair of himself or of others ; he believes everything and he hopes everything. Christian hope would seem to be naïve, but only in human eyes. In reality the hope that hopes everything creates conditions conducive to a change of heart and a change in circumstances. Since a Christian's invicible hope has complete confidence in God, it also has confidence in every person and this transfigures situations and events. For the Christian possessed by hope, all is grace, even difficulties and suffering, for they develop faith and charity. Christian hope begets fundamental optimism.

Charity, the fruit of faith is generous love, sacrificing itself for God and for others. Charity, St. Paul considers to be the greatest of all. Indeed, faith and hope will cease, when we are gathered in the Kingdom of God for life eternal; charity alone, love for God and love for man will endure eternally. God is love; love is the expression of the very being of God, and therefore love is eternal. In the first place charity binds us to God. This love of God cannot be separated from love of all people. Jesus summed up all the Law when he said : "You shall love the Lord your God with all your heart, with all your soul and with all your mind. This is the first commandment and the greatest; the second is like it : You shall love your neighbour as yourself" (Matt. 22. 37-39).

Love for one's neighbour, the person we live with or the person we meet, whoever it is, means loving God in him. Christ present or prefigured in him : that is why the first and second commandments of Christ are alike. God cannot be loved in faith and prayer alone, he must also be loved in others. And this neighbour, this other, must be loved as one's self. Christ in his boundless compassion proposes a commandment of love, which lies within our capacity. Since we know how, and how much, we love ourselves, Christ proposes that we should give our neighbour at least the same love we have for ourselves. The love of Christian charity is made up of sacrifice and generosity. We have to forget ourselves and see ourselves in the other person in order to give ourselves to him with full generosity. Charity does not seek its own satisfaction, but solely the good and the joy of the other person; in this generous sacrifice we find our true selves, our hearts expand to the proportions of the love of Christ and we find our own greatest happiness at the same time as our neighbour's, the other person we have loved as ourselves, and also loved for God, who loves him and is visible in him.

The source of Christian life is life in Christ by faith, hope and charity. For the Christian the whole of life stems from this. But it is obvious that outside of this life in Christ, which generates faith, hope and charity, human lives exist which sometimes resemble the Christian life. It is possible for people who do not know Christ to show the characteristics of Christian morality. "When the pagans, who do not have the Law, do naturally what the Law commands", writes St. Paul, "they are a law to themselves... Their conduct shows that what the Law requires is written on their hearts..." (Romans 2. 14-15).

By this, God demonstrates that he does not leave any of his creatures in disorder. Although faith in Christ does not possess a man's heart, he is nevertheless preserved and sustained by the providence of God, who writes in his heart elements of the moral law to protect him, and to prevent him from falling into complete disorder. Certainly, man can still stifle this voice of conscience and reject the law written in his heart. He is judged then, under the judgement of this law, which comes secretly from God. So, each one is judged according to the law he knows, the Christian on his faithfulness to the commands of Christ, the Jew by the law of Moses, and the pagan by the law in his inmost heart.

This law, inscribed in the heart of man, gives him the moral conscience which can make him perform actions worthy of a Christian. If such a man obeys the inner law, he can even demonstrate more integrity than a Christian whose life does not conform to his beliefs. The Church should have the greatest respect for those upright men, who, without any knowledge of Christ, obey their conscience, for she should discern in them the very work of God, who has written a moral law in their hearts to preserve them and to prepare them. However, this conscience and this moral obedience are not enough to lead them to that peace which can only be found in the knowledge of Jesus Christ. The law inscribed on their hearts preserves them only from moral disorder, gives them a human dignity which relates them to Christians and prepares them to receive the fullness of life in Christian faith, hope and charity. However, if they do not follow the moral law written on their hearts, this law is their judge and reveals their guilt, which can only be removed in the forgiveness received from Jesus Christ.

So the Church must have a very broad attitude towards all, for she knows that the law written on their hearts cannot so easily be obeyed without the knowledge and love of Christ. The Church is filled with wonder to see so many good people outside her communion, people who lead honourable lives and manifest the providence of God ; but she passes no judgement on so many people who cannot obey their consciences, for she knows that only the grace of Christ can give a person strength and courage to persevere, that only the love of Christ can give reasonable grounds and effective motivation for a constant and faithful life.

The Christian life is a balanced, liberated life, sometimes running the risk of two contradictory temptations : puritanism and permissiveness. On the one hand the Christian life implies certain breaks with natural, sinful life ; the Christian is to live in the world, without belonging to the world. However, these breaks tend sometimes to become generalised. The Christian then runs the risk of thinking that the more faithful he is, the more he will cut himself off from the world, and be separate from sinful men (as if he himself were not still a sinner as well), and live a life claiming to be pure of all contact with those still in the clutches of sin. On the other hand, the Christian life implies a presence in the world and a freedom in charity. But this presence and this freedom may make the Christian run the risk of being recaptured by the spirit of the world and by the attraction of his own self-will. The Christian risks believing he is more human and more free if he passes no judgement on sin, shares totally in the anguish and questioning of this world, and lives a life which pretends to be free of all complexes and all taboos.

A Christian life is neither puritan nor permissive ; it consists of breaks and detachments which are necessary with regard to natural, sinful life, but is completely human and free in everything which must not of necessity be avoided or rejected. The Christian is as human as everyone else is, distinguished only by charity, which implies sacrifice where he is concerned and kindness where everyone else is concerned, in the liberty of those who know no law but that of love for God and one's neighbours. This balance is not easily kept ; it is not always simple to see clearly what attitude we should take in certain circumstances. The judgement of the universal Christian community is more sure that that of the local community or the individual. That is why the individual should keep to the attitude of the Church, even if he does not always see that it is justified, or if he thinks that it can evolve further in faithfulness to God's word.

Christian life as a whole is contained and summed up in charity, sacrificial, generous love for God and neighbour. St. Paul names charity as the first fruit of the Holy Spirit in the heart, later he shows all the implications of charity, in the list of the fruits of the Spirit (Gal. 5. 22-23), and in the hymn to charity (1 Cor. 13. 4-7). These two texts,

154

which overlap on certain points, sum up the whole
of Christian teaching on living.

We will simply follow the list of the fruits of
the Spirit, completed by the hymn to charity, high-
lighting the various aspects of life presented in these
two texts. There is no order of precedence in the
fruits of the Spirit or of charity. They rise spont-
aneously as the apostle's meditation develops. All are
of equal importance and each demonstrates, in its
own way, what is the love in charity of the faithful
Christian.

"The fruits of the Spirit are love, joy, peace,
patience, kindness, goodness, trust, gentleness and
self-control" (Gal. 5. 22-23).

"Love is patient ; love is kind and envies no one ;
love is never boastful, conceited nor rude ; never
selfish, never quick to take offence ; love is not resent-
ful, love takes no delight in wrong but delights in
the truth. Love bears all things ; believes all things ;
hopes all things" (1 Cor. 13. 4-7).

From these two passages we can see emerging
the fruits of charity :

joy and peace,
patience and kindness,
goodness and trust,
gentleness and self-control,
moderation and humility,
poverty and purity,
generosity and mercy,
justice and truth.

32

JOY AND PEACE

Joy is the Christian attitude which displays our faith in the resurrection of Christ, the conqueror of evil and death, and our hope in the resurrection of all who believe, to life eternal in God's Kingdom. The source of our Christian joy is therefore the Easter victory. It is because he is certain of Christ's victory over death and of his power over the world, that the Christian can always be fundamentally joyful even under difficulties and in suffering. The Christian lives as a person risen from the dead, endowed with the power of a victory over evil and suffering. He can therefore never completely lose heart.

Christian joy, grounded in our faith in the resurrection, lifts us out of ourselves, our difficulties and our distress, and transports us into contemplation of Christ's glory; it gives us detachment from the saddening world of sin, and lets us savour the joy of the unseen world, of the saints gathered around their risen Lord. It is our life hidden with Christ in God which arouses and sustains our joy. Christian joy is eschatological, too; it is set afire by the prospect of the glorious return of Christ. This joy banishes care from our hearts and makes us want to pray. The quiet simple witness of this joy is an impressive sign of the presence of Christ within us ; Christ who is our life and our joy. This joy, even in suffering and difficulties, is proof of the victory of the risen Christ in us, and leads others to glorify God.

But Christian joy does not come easily ; it is the fruit of faith's warfare against the powers of evil, that seize upon our wounded personalities and keep trying to sadden us. There are days when we feel distressed and miserable, when we only want to hide away and weep over ourselves. But the joy of Christ is at hand, watching over us in the person of someone else, a joy that lifts us out of loneliness and anxiety, and brings us to the festival of God's King-dom, where the company of Christ's Saints sings and rejoices.

Christian joy is also communion with all man-kind, communion with them in their hopes, their happiness and their festivities, marvelling at creation and all the beauty of human life, showing in this way that Christ is completely human with all human beings. Did he not compare the communion of the Kingdom of God to a great wedding banquet ? Did he not share his joy and eat with publicans and sinners in Levi's home ? Christian joy, so completely human, is the answer to the distress and sadness of so many people who are unconsciously waiting for Christians to give them a sign of communion and compassion, a hope of true happiness, through the serene joy that is theirs, shining with the presence of Christ.

Peace is sister to joy, for peace too springs from certainty of the resurrection and the kingship of Christ. No disaster is capable of shattering the Chris-tian now, for he has entrusted himself completely to the love of Christ. St Paul writes : "Never be anxious about anything, but in every need turn to prayer and intercession with thanksgiving ; and lay your requests before God. And the peace of God which is beyond comprehension will keep your heart and mind in Christ Jesus" (Phil. 4. 6-7). In his life of prayer the Christian nourishes in his heart the peace which comes from God. He can confide everything and entrust everything to Christ, his cares, his anxieties and his problems, certain that God in his compassion will take charge of it all and give the best solution. So he can wait in peace, even when the answer to his prayer is not given at once. In this peace, sustained by prayer, the Christian's personality, often fragmented by the events and temptations of life, is brought once more into unity.

Peace arises from the reconciliation of the individual with God and with himself. We are often wounded by life, so that we find it difficult to accept ourselves as we are. We are inclined to judge ourselves severely, to dwell morbidly on our so-called unworthiness, creating a weighty guilt-complex, denying our human nature, our affectivity, our sexuality and our aggressivity... The peace regained in prayer gradually effects an inner reconciliation of all these divergent and often warring tendencies. Peace makes it possible to accept ourselves as we are ; to master our wounded nature and bring into harmony mind and will, heart and body, simply and freely submitting them to the love of God and of neighbour, confessing whatever is really sinful in us so that God can forgive us, and rejoicing in God's gift of sensitivity which can be a real means of communion with others.

The Christian is a person of inward peace who radiates and creates peace. One of the Beatitudes pronounced by Jesus declares : "Happy the peacemakers, for they will be called sons of God" (Matt. 5. 9). The Christian who radiates peace, creates peace and generates peace about him, is worthy of the title given to Christ himself : he is called son of God. This work of peace may be accomplished in various fields : among the people about us, in relation to the problems of war in the world, in relation to the visible unity of all Christians...

The Christian who by his life of prayer discovers inner peace and sustains it, makes it possible by his peaceful attitude, for his neighbour to find that same inner peace ; it is part of Christian charity so to transmit the peace of Christ to others that they may be drawn to it, finding peace with God and with themselves, and regaining their inner unity. The Christian also creates peace among the people about him ; he anticipates or heals discord, quarrels and disputes ; he is never glad when divisions arise between people ; he prefers above all else peace and unity.

With regard to the problem of war, the Christian must at all costs be militant for peace. War is never a solution to any political or social problem. There is no such thing as a just war. Certainly a Christian may be called to defend the people he lives with against unavoidable external violence. But for him this kind of defence against violence is a necessity which brings no lasting solution ; reconciliation and peace among men are the only effective solutions because they are positive. The Christian must be an apostle of peace among the nations, peace which may demand the most costly sacrifices, for it is paramount that war be avoided at all costs, war being the most hideous form of human pride. The Christian can only accept the army as a policing force in the service of peace, which should gradually become more and more useless. For some Christians conscientious objection is a form of vocation.

Within the Church, among divided Christians there is also a work of peace, to bring about the visible unity of all : it is called ecumenism. The Christian desires, as Christ himself prayed, that all should recover visible unity in one single Church. He cannot consider that the divisions between Christians and the schism in the Church are justified and permanent. He dislikes polemics and proselytizing : If he has to declare his beliefs, he does so with a profound understanding for the point of view held by other Christians. Such an understanding implies neither denial of his own beliefs nor a confusion of the issues involved, rather it springs from a spirit of peace, which pleads for unity of faith at points where people can still see nothing but opposition or divergence. Such a Christian does not seek to win other Christians over to his point of view, for he trusts the Holy Spirit who alone can convince the heart of the truth of Christ. If he has to witness to his beliefs, he does so with deep respect for the freedom of conscience of others. The truth of Christ requires neither political constraint, nor proselytizing to win its victory in peace ; it is in peace and gentleness that the Holy Spirit acts through the word of God to lead us into the full light of Christ ; he has no need of human power and agitation. Evangelisation is peaceful witness to the truth, with a spirit intent on the unity of all Christians.

Peace surpasses our understanding ; peace is the very presence of Christ, our peace, in us and among us. If we allow ourselves to be possessed by this mystery of God's peace, our hearts and our thoughts are sure of being truly kept under its protection, in communion with the very heart and mind of Jesus Christ himself.

33

PATIENCE AND KINDNESS

The patience of Christian love is forbearance, magnanimity, endurance and perseverance. If joy and peace spring from faith in the resurrection, patience is communion with the sufferings of Christ. According to St. Paul charity is patient (1 Cor. 13. 4), that is to say, a Christian's love for God and for others is a sacrificial love, forgetfulness of self, giving one's self to others, in imitation of the love of Christ in his passion and on the cross.

Christ was patient. Patience and passion (in the sense of love and suffering), have the same derivation. Christ loved us to the point of suffering and dying for us with the greatest patience. The love of charity involves suffering in patience. Charity is not love in terms of exclusive possession, but love in terms of generous sacrifice, so it is ready to suffer patiently. Suffering purifies love, which can sometimes run the risk of becoming narrowly possessive. Suffering reminds us that our love for others has to be a forgetting of self, a free and generous gift. Patience means confidently awaiting the joy and peace of God after suffering. Since the resurrection of Christ, a Christian knows that there is no suffering which does not lead to perfect joy ; that is why he is patient, calm and paceful, knowing that God, in his good time, will let him savour the perfect joy of charity. We cannot omit any of these stages willed by God ; we cannot attain happiness by our own efforts ; God alone holds the secret of our happiness and of the right time for its fulfilment. A Christian is called to wait patiently for joy to come, and that teaches him total dependence upon God, poor in human resources, but sure that the strength of God is made perfect in our weakness.

Christ was magnanimous. A Christian is long-suffering with himself and with others ; he too is magnanimous. He is not severe on others ; he is not impatient to see them adopt his own point of view, even if he considers it better ; he is not impatient for others to develop in ways which will help his relationship with them ; he readily forgives their faults, knowing that the love of Christ covers a multitude of sins. And for his opponents he will have the generosity of Christ who prayed for his executioners : "Father, forgive them. They know not what they do" (Luke 23. 24).

Patience is also endurance. A Christian is courageous, knowing that his faith makes demands on him and can put him in difficult situations in the world, even persecution, and possibly martyrdom. His patient charity is ready to endure anything for the love of God and his neighbours. In some circumstances, he may be tempted to modify the demands of his faith to avoid difficulties ; when he does so he knows that he is failing in true Christian love, for he has stopped witnessing to Christ crucified and is now unable to help his fellow-men. Certainly, it is not always easy for the Christian to know how far he can go in accepting the demands of this world, of a human authority or of a concrete situation, without forfeiting the purity of his faith and compromising the clear light of his witnessing. An excessive insistence on the faith can also constitute a useless hindrance to Christian witness ; in the end it can damage both truth and charity. A Christian has to keep a balance between faith which is true to necessary essentials and charity which, in matters of secondary importance, is free. But in any case, a Christian is ready to endure in faith and in charity, which may involve sharing, in his own body, in the cross of Christ.

Finally, patience is perseverance. To anyone who has to sustain the warfare of Christian living, life often seems long. He may say with St. Paul "I am caught in this dilemma : on the one hand, I want to go and be with Christ, which would be better by far ; on the other, to live on here in my body is more urgent for your sake" (Phil. 1. 23-24). The Christian lives in this tension : he longs for the end of life's struggle, when death unites him peacefully with Christ, or when his Lord returns in his glory to raise him up to life eternal ; and he also longs for life's joy to continue, for the happiness of those around him. But in this tension, he commits himself entirely to God, who knows which is the better course, and who for the difficulties of our struggle grants graces more than sufficient. The Christian has to be ready to persevere in the battle of the Christian life over a long period of time, and he must arm himself for the fight each day in renewed faith, hope, love and prayer. Persevering in this way, he discovers the joy of deep communion with his brothers, who, like himself, or more than himself, have to battle on in this world in order to persevere to the end which comes at an hour known only to God. This perseverance, patterned on that of Christ along the way of the cross, gives the Christian the chance of sharing in the prolonged suffering of so many who do not have the hope of Christ to light their hard road. And in persevering thus, the Christian finds joy in being so fully with others that he can help them along the long road of life.

Kindness is the dedication and eagerness proper to charity. The Christian is the servant of God and of others. Christian love is kind (1 Cor. 13. 4). Christ made himself the servant of his followers. A dispute had arisen among the apostles to determine which of them should be considered the greatest. Jesus said to them : "Let the greatest of you behave like the youngest, and your leader like a servant... Here am I among you, a servant" (Luke 22. 26-27).

Following the example of Christ, the Christian has to become the servant of his brothers and of all mankind. He cannot consider himself the greatest, or a great man among others, but he has always to show himself dedicated and eager to serve others. Even if he holds authority, he must consider it as a service and behave as if he were the youngest member of the Christian community. To govern, it is important to know how to serve, and high office in the Church is a humble way of serving others. The Christian is both witness and sign of the Servant Christ among his friends and colleagues.

In the action of washing his apostles' feet, on the eve of his passion, Christ gave kindness its full spiritual dimension. The washing of the feet is a sign of Christ's ministry as servant ; each Christian has to accomplish in life the kind of service of which Christ gave the example. The washing of feet is a sign of humble Christian love and a sharing in the ministry of Christ. When the Church acts out this sign in the liturgy of Holy Thursday she sings : "Where love and charity are, there is God." Service, here symbolised by the washing of feet is a sign of the presence of the servant — Christ. It is also a sign of being part of God's work in Jesus Christ. To Peter who was unwilling to accept the gesture, Christ said, "If I do not wash you, you have no part in me" (John 13. 8). The Christian whose ministry is to hold authority in the Church must realise that those he is charged to lead, cannot share the concerns of his ministry or accept him wholeheartedly, unless he is their dedicated, eager servant, showing his willingness to serve them as his Master served. Such humble service is the sign of sharing the authority of Christ.

By their spirit of service in humble charity, those holding authority in the Church show that their authority comes from the servant-Christ, who washed his disciples' feet. In addition, he keeps his authority brotherly, simple and approachable. Those to whom he ministers, feel confident, because they are not dominated, but led with understanding, served humbly, and loved personally; they have a share in the responsibilities and concerns of his authority, with hearts ready to serve in their turn. So, authority in the Church partakes of the authority of the servant-Christ, and brings others to share in the same service of God and man.

By kindness, a Christian shares in the humility and the service of Christ, which culminated in the humiliation and sacrifice of the cross. Like patience, kindness is a communion in the passion of Christ for all mankind.

34

GOODNESS AND TRUST

Goodness is the human face of charity. St. Paul instances goodness as the first fruit of light : "Once you were in darkness, but now you are light in the Lord ; live as children of light ; for the fruit of the light is all goodness, justice and truth" (Eph. 5. 8-9). By goodness, the Christian gives expression to the light of charity in human forms and attitudes. Charity can sometimes seem superhuman, difficult to achieve, beyond our reach. But by his goodness the Christian proves how near it really lies.

Joy and peace have their source in faith in the resurrection. Patience and kindness are a sharing in the patience and humility of Christ in his passion ; goodness and trust are founded upon the mystery of the incarnation. Since the love of Christ was incarnate in simple human love, since Christ trusted the men who wanted to follow him, in spite of the complications of their sinfulness, the Christian reveals the love of charity in goodness and trust.

Christian goodness is a human quality transfigured and deepened by charity. Goodness is welcoming, simple, uncritical and childlike. It removes from growing Christian holiness all that might seem hard or inhuman ; it rids others of the illusion that a Christian is someone special, no longer subject to temptations or problems. Goodness, which is so

understanding of others, brings charity within everybody's reach, strips holiness of its austerity and gives
a human face to conduct which is most strictly
faithful to the will of Christ.

Goodness is the humour in Christian living. By
his goodness, the Christian appears as he really is,
without falling into vulgarity and without playing
down God's demands. Goodness makes a Christian
able to laugh at himself, when he is inclined to
take himself too seriously or to exaggerate his own
importance. It is goodness that strips our awareness
of sin of any unhealthy excesses ; for morbid guilt
it substitutes simple repentance ; it laughs at the
powers of evil, which have been overcome by the
risen Christ.

St. Paul expresses the significance of Christian
goodness when he says of charity that it forgives
everything and believes everything (1 Cor. 13. 7).
Goodness demands much of itself, but closes its eyes
to the faults of others, convinced as it is that love
covers a multitude of sins and that it cannot criticize
those whom God alone has the right to judge. Besides,
the goodness of charity is more effective than any
amount of judging to bring someone to necessary
repentance : goodness forgives everything. Goodness
is childlike ; so convinced of the power of God to
bring everybody, even the greatest hypocrites, to be
honest with themselves and others ; so sure that
acts of sincere love are effective that it considers
mankind as virtually won over already for God and
for right. In this it anticipates the conversion of
hearts which it affects : goodness believes everything.

Trust, which is one form of faith in God, is
optimism about people, in spite of the devious ways
of their hearts. Christ gives his trust to all to whom
he shows his love, for he knows that by the Holy
Spirit, even the opposition in our hearts can turn

into consent. The Christian too trusts his neighbour ; as St. Paul says, he never gives up hope in another, and he will endure anything from him (1 Cor. 13. 7). Really, man always remains a mystery and we can never be rationally certain of what a person thinks or feels. In some sense we also have to believe in man, believe that God is powerful enough, and his grace effective enough, for what we are expecting from another to exist, really and definitively, in his heart ; so by trust, faith in man and in his identity with ourselves, we are ready to endure in our relationships all kinds of disappointments, resulting from outward appearances, and to hope for all kinds of victories, promises of reality.

Even the most fulfilled love and the most intimate friendship do not of themselves convey absolute and definitive certainty about the feelings and the loyalty of another person. The deepest and most enlightening exchanges leave us with a degree of solitude and comparative anxiety as regards the other. Marriage does not of itself provide a solution to the solitude and the anxiety. Yet, by trusting, man can begin to believe in man, and to be certain that a reality underlies his words, that his thoughts and his heart are indeed as he says. And, even if his words go beyond what is strictly true, the trust of the other lovingly constrains him to be in reality what he says.

Trust is the health of all human relationships, of love and friendship. Without trust, relationships become restless and anxious. Man is always demanding fresh signs of the reality of love, and he cannot be satisfied if he does not believe as much as he sees. This demand for proof, which can become morbid is often the cause of difficulties in marriage and sexual life.

But anyone who comes to trust in another emerges from loneliness and anxiety. By the strength trust gives, he strengthens those sentiments he believes to exist in the other on the basis of words and signs which have been freely bestowed, not passionately demanded. He can rely on the positive impressions he has received, for they are sure to be correct if he has been able to sustain an atmosphere of creative, life-giving trust. Then he can believe everything and hope everything of the other ; this is no illusion, but confidence in the reality existing and alive in the mind and heart of the other person, however clumsily expressed. Anyone who has experienced this real confidence is no longer alone and anxious, for now he can believe that the other and he are really alike, in suffering and in joy.

Genuine trust believes everything and hopes everything of the other and this makes it possible to excuse everything and endure everything arising from his failings. If the other, through my trusting becomes like myself, I can believe and hope in him, in his feelings and in his thoughts, as much as I believe and hope in myself ; I can excuse everything, and endure everything from the other, without ceasing to believe everything and hope everything of him, since I excuse and endure myself, without losing trust and hope in myself. As I know myself, I can know the other too, and trust him just as I trust myself. This is to apply Christ's command : "You shall love your neighbour as yourself." Jealousy of heart, which so often disturbs close relationships between people and makes them suffer from imaginary signs of infidelity, can only be set at rest by that trust which believes, hopes, excuses and endures everything.

35

GENTLENESS AND SELF-CONTROL

Gentleness of heart and self-control are two complementary and balancing aspects of Christian personality. "Take my yoke upon you" said Christ, "and learn from me, for I am gentle and humble of heart" (Matt. 11. 29). And St. Paul exhorts Christians : "Keep alert, stand firm in the faith, be courageous, be strong. Let all you do be done in love" (1 Cor. 16. 13-14). Gentleness of heart is a courageous gentleness ; self-control a strength filled with gentleness.

Gentleness is refusal to give way to violence, anger and irritation. Charity is not irritable (1 Cor. 13. 5), for anger is a product of the flesh (Gal. 5. 20). Christ showed anger against a neighbour to be equivalent to murder, which is condemned by the ten commandments of God (Matt. 5. 20-24). Violence, anger, bad temper, even in words, arise from the same source in our hearts as murder. They come from a refusal to accept the existence of a neighbour as he is, and therefore from a secret desire to destroy him with wounding word or harsh gestures, since social restraints stop us from eliminating him by actual murder.

Violence has a deep psychological root in our

hearts — aggression, which is a perverted form, of self-assertion. Our personality needs to define itself both by opposition to another and by defending itself against him. Aggression makes us forget that our personality, which has every right to assert itself in human society, can only do so effectively and permanently when it is certain that victory is already won, without any need of violence. The Christian knows that God has loved him, chosen him and saved him personally, that God has so established his personality, in its unique character, in a domain which need not be defended, because it is his for ever. Each individual is so precious in God's sight that he has a unique vocation before him, a function which is irreplaceable, a position which is impregnable. He has therefore no need to fight, or to defend himself in order to assert a personality which God loves particulary, and strengthens progressively according to his will. Aggression in a Christian's heart is sublimated by the certainty that he is a child of God, loved, led and personally strengthened as a unique, irreplaceable being, established in his own impregnable domain.

Gentleness is an attitude of non-violence. Christ won the greatest of all victories by gentleness, in his life and in his passion. He was treated atrociously, but he humbled himself without opening his mouth, like a lamb led to the slaughter, and a sheep dumb before the shearers (Isa. 54.7). The Christian is called to follow the same way of non-violence, certain as he is of winning every victory with Christ by gentleness alone. His struggle is for God's peace, and this peace can be won, for oneself or for others, only in gentleness. Violence can impose a power or an opinion temporarily but it does not produce obedience or conviction. Only non-violent gentleness can enter the depths of the human heart and bring people to obey Christ and convince them of the truth. In his legitimate demands for justice, a Christian will always prefer non-violence, as a sign of the victorious gentleness of Christ. He will always choose Christ's methods rather than those of violent revolution leading to bloodshed. Not that a Christian should be passive, take a conservative or reactionary stand and condone human situations, political or social, which are intolerable, because they contradict the justice of God. Since the victory of the cross, which brought joy for all the world, the Christian is convinced of the unique persuasive power of gentleness in non-violence. So it is for a more effective and more lasting revolution that he chooses the weapons of non-violent gentleness.

"Happy the gentle", proclaims Christ, "for they will inherit the Promised Land" (Matt. 5. 4). Not only spiritual victory is promised to gentleness, but real power over earthly realities. The gentle who intend to struggle and convince by non-violence, gradually become the true inheritors of the earth. They will have the final say on authorities and injustices in this world, and will prepare in effective and lasting peace the coming of the Kingdom of God.

Self-control balances gentleness, keeps it from becoming sentimental and preserves its virility and strength. It is the mastery a Christian acquires over his whole personality, his thinking, feelings, will and body. This mastery is not produced by his own human effort, but by the power of the Holy Spirit within him, invoked and sought in the life of prayer. Of course, personal effort is required in spiritual discipline to help the whole being to consent to the commands of the Holy Spirit. But at its source and throughout this striving, the Christian always recognises the supernatural action of God, so that he can attribute nothing to himself that has not been given him by Christ.

The Christian works with discipline and enthusiasm for the completion of his salvation ; but, as St. Paul says, he knows that God is there, in the striving instigated by the Holy Spirit, transmitting the energy which leads him both to will and to do, for the fulfilment of God's purposes (Phil. 2. 12-13). Christian spiritual discipline, having as its goal complete self-mastery, therefore essentially involves consenting to the power of the Holy Spirit, who gives the strength to will and to act in conformity with God's commands.

Self-control gives a Christian a balanced outlook, one that does not choose extreme positions from a spirit of contradiction, but discerns wisely what is good and positive in every opinion, discarding all that is negative or wrong. Self-mastery also involves our feelings ; the Christian seeks to master his passions, and never make of any of God's creatures an idol who might gradually come to usurp the place of Christ in his heart. A Christian also trains his will, applying disciplines which will dispose it to consent more readily to the actions God commands and the breaks with the past he requires. Finally, the Christian disciplines his body to obey the rules of prayer and sanctification so that it may be transfigured by the inner flame of charity.

36

MODERATION AND HUMILITY

Moderation is control over the body and the emotions. According to St. Paul, love neither covets nor envies, and is not jealous (1 Cor. 13. 4). Charity accepts a certain disciplining of the body and the emotions to be more true and generous, and develops a spirit of self-sacrifice with the senses held in check. Our bodies and our emotions bind us closely to the created order, and by attaching us excessively to the natural life, they can hinder our union with God and the gift of ourselves to others. They tend to turn us in upon ourselves, and make us seek our own ends for selfish satisfaction. Moderation is therefore a discipline reminding the body and the emotions that they too are instruments for the glory of God in our lives.

In obedience to God's command, the Christian must guard against covetousness or envy, which can impair the legitimate desires of his body : food, sexuality ; or of his feelings : acquisitiveness, affectivity. The Christian can freely enjoy the good things of creation. "To the pure all things are pure... Whoever eats is honouring the Lord, for he gives thanks to God. Indeed no one among us lives for himself, as no one dies for himself ; if we live, it is for the Lord, and if we die, we die for the Lord. And so, living or dying, we belong to the Lord" (Titus 1. 15, Rom. 14. 6-8). Eating is a legitimate enjoyment for the Christian, a very human enjoyment and an occasion of thanksgiving to God for his creation. But the Christian can exercise control over his body by moderation, sometimes even by abstinence or fasting. Fasting is a sign of our freedom regarding the things of creation ; it is an offering of our bodies, signifying that God is amply sufficient for us and satisfies us completely : it is a sharing of the passion of Christ, a placing of ourselves at the disposal of the Holy Spirit in meditation on the Word of God ; our true and living bread.

Fasting relates not only to food ; it can also be temporary abstinence from a pleasure which attaches us too much to the world and causes us to forget the only true joy, Christ. Moderation in speech is also necessary. We sometimes tend to talk too much and give inordinate expression to wishes or anxieties : a certain silence can remind us that God alone really knows and understands our problems, giving peace in prayer. But silence must not mean withdrawal from communion with people ; on the contrary, temporary silence and retreat, fasting from speech, are a means of reviving our love for others and preparing to express our love more deeply and truly.

In life as in death, in the life of the senses as in fasting the senses, we are the Lord's and all should be done with thanksgiving. The Christian must discover the balance between enjoyment of the things of this world and temporary detachment from them. The sign of this balance is thanksgiving : if the Christian remains joyful, thanking God for making him as he his, he has found balance in the life of the senses.

Moderation has also to govern human sexuality and the urge to possess ; we will touch on these aspects of moderation later when we speak of poverty and purity. Moderation is also a discipline of our human emotions. The need for love and affection, the dread of loneliness and abandonment, sometimes exacerbate our legitimate emotions. We have seen how trust can balance this longing for affection. Moderation should also help us to accept something less than that absolute of ultimate satisfaction we always dream about but can never attain. Only the love of Christ can finally satisfy ; and only the human love that is willing to sacrifice itself generously for another, using the simplest words and signs, can also give the human heart a fullness of joy. There is an abstinence from emotional expression which renews it and opens the way to sure and certain joy, without the illusion of absolute and ultimate satisfaction which is impossible. Only the resurrection will give us love fulfilled in eternal satisfaction.

Humility is the realisation that God is all ; that the human self is nothing, of no account except by the gifts that God has given, directly or through others. Christian humility is not annihilation of the personality, but the certainty that God comes into the very depths of our misery to find us ; to be raised up with him we have to humble ourselves and find him by abandoning all pride. The Christian has no illusions about himself ; his conviction of being simply wretched and weak reminds him that he has everything to expect and ask from God. Pride is an illusion of the self which always considers itself better than it really is. Humility is the realistic view the Christian takes of himself.

If the Christian strives for humility, he finds Christ there, and he raises him up with himself. The strength of God is fulfilled in human weakness. Humility does not destroy the personality ; on the contrary, it is the means of discovering the way of true power, the power of God which acts in our weakness. Anyone who, in humility, accepts to lose his life, a life built upon selfishness and pride, recovers true life through the power of God, life which is the life of Christ filling his whole being.

Humility also recognises the superiority of the Christian community, the Church, over the individual. The Christian considers others to be better than himself, for he knows his own weakness and rejoices in his neighbour's sanctification. Still, the Christian is not ungrateful towards God. He knows that Christ is alive within him and that the Holy Spirit fills him with his gifts ; he has to thank God the Father for that, humbly, as for a present not deserved. At the same time, he knows how firmly selfishness and pride are rooted in his heart ; that is why he is always ready to acknowledge that others are of more value than he.

Humility, which gives the glory to God and rejoices to see his work in others, brings the Christian into true obedience. Since he knows himself to be incapable of any good thing without God, he longs to submit to him in all things and allow God to lead him according to his will. He knows that the authority and the will of God are represented by the spiritual authorities who fulfil their office in the Church. The Christian obeys his spiritual leaders, since they are watching over the salvation of his soul, for which they will have to give account (Heb. 13. 17). He obeys them, not as human beings but as ambassadors and instruments of Christ himself. In them he discerns the word of God, directing him into the sure paths of truth and of love. This obedience does not imply the suppression of personal judgment. It is possible for the Christian to disagree with the person who has authority over him ; he can keep his own judgment ; but he obeys, in order to train himself in the obedience of Christ and to maintain the unity of the Christian community. For those in authority in the Church are instruments of Christ in the service of unity in love.

37

POVERTY AND PURITY

Poverty is the Christian's conviction that he is dependent on God alone. It is a feeling of emptiness that only Christ can fill with his fullness. Poverty rejects the securities that this world may give, in order to display the one and only security which is in God. It is a detachment from property, possessions and power, signifying that all things are God's. The Christian considers himself a steward of all that belongs to God.

"Happy the poor in heart, the Kingdom of Heaven is theirs" (Matt. 5. 3). The spirit of poverty, of detachment from personal property, power and ownership, prepares the Christian to take possession of the greatest of all good things which alone can satisfy him, the joy of the Kingdom of God. This fullness of joy is given only to those who are ready to give up everything for love of Christ and their neighbour.

The Christian spirit of poverty, which exposes him to possible material poverty, does not make him more ready to accept other people's poverty. On the contrary, the Christian has to be militant for the improvement of social and economic conditions for the whole society. The spirit of poverty makes him want to share with others whatever material or spiritual wealth God has given him. The Christian is in favour of all community patterns of work and of living which ensure a fair distribution of the good things of the earth to everybody.

Purity is the will to faithful love. Purity of heart is sincerity, chastity and simplicity. Its source is in our love for Christ ; he it is who, by his abounding love for us, can give us true sincerity of heart in our love for him and for others. Purity of heart makes the Christian faithful in charity and in human love.

The heart of man, in all its complications, is often tempted to variation and to unfaithfulness in love. Because of sin, man is not naturally constant in his human love. It is the love of charity, self-sacrificing and generous, creating purity of heart, which can give him sincerity, constancy and faithfulness in love ; without this there can be nothing but disorder, disgust and despair.

Chastity, the fruit of purity of heart, is mastery of the sexual and emotional life. The Christian is not called to suppress by puritanical restraint, the aspirations of his powers of loving. He knows, however, that if these powers are uncontrolled, they will cause disorder in his heart and excessive attachment to the physical expressions of love. Chastity in marriage is a conscious understanding between husband and wife ; such an understanding may imply for both some degree of sacrifice, which has to be accepted by each as an act of self-giving, a mortification of selfishness in order to give true joy, as the other requires. Chastity in celibacy is inspired by the conviction that our powers of loving can bear all the more spiritual fruit, in charity, in contemplative life and in the service of others, when they are not exhausted in selfish gratification which turns man in upon himself. We must not exaggerate the sexual problem in life. We have to remember that our personality, often wounded, keeps urging us to prove our ability to love, and this can constitute a temptation. It is union with Christ in prayer, in generous giving of ourselves to others, in service and in sacrifice, which strengthens us in chastity, and prevents our self-seeking, keeping us strong and free to be available in love and in service of Christ. Confession and the Eucharist are effective aids in preserving purity of heart in chastity.

Finally, purity of heart is simplicity. To the Christian, love for Christ and for others is a simple love, which flees complications and all devious paths. The Christian has to be frank and direct in his relationships with others ; but out of love for his neighbour, and respect for his feelings, he exercises all the refinements of tact, rather than wound another. Charity is discreet and makes no parade of the difficulties which arise between people, although it is frank and simple ; it prompts the Christian to resolve peacefully and simply the differences which might otherwise separate him from others. The Christian simplifies everything around him : his material existence, his dealings with others, his plans and his ambitions. All he needs to realise is the one essential — love for God and for others ; for him the rest has only relative importance.

"Happy the pure in heart, they will see God" (Matt. 5. 8). Purity of heart, sincerity, chastity and simplicity are promised the vision of God. The eyes of those whose hearts are not divided — between the true love of charity which quickens human loving and the urge to gratify selfish desires — are completely focused on God, simply attentive in prayer and contemplation. They will enter directly into the Kingdom of God, for they will already be accustomed to seeing Christ in the purity of a simple heart, in the life of prayer and in their brothers and sisters.

38

GENEROSITY AND MERCY

The generosity of charity is the Christian's refusal to seek self-satisfaction in any matter whatever
(1 Cor. 13. 5); on the contrary, the Christian opens
his heart and shares with his neighbour in every
situation. Generosity expresses itself in brotherly
love, hospitality and warm-hearted giving.

We all tend to regard ourselves as isolated
individuals, and try to defend our personality, our
independence and our interest. The generosity of
charity opens us to life in community with others.
The Christian then considers himself a humble member of the Body of Christ, the Church, and of the
whole human community. He knows that God is
working through his people all over the world, of
which he is but a modest unit. What matters to him
is that God's work should be done in the world by
all God's servants, not that his own selfish rights
and his own particular powers should be defended
and justified. The Christian sees himself as a willing
instrument in God's hands and he is glad, if others
seem to be of more use than he is.

Generosity develops the spirit of brotherhood.
As all Christians are brothers and sisters in God's
family, it matters little who is chosen by God to
do his work. What matters is that God's work is
done, not that it should be done by me. Jealousy
between Christians or between communities in the

Church is a cancer, and history is full of its unedifying consequences. How can a Christian, who seeks only the glory of God and the accomplishment of his work, be jealous of a neighbour because he seems more favoured or more successful than he ? To be delivered from jealousy, which is meanness of heart, a Christian has to nourish within himself a spirit of brotherly love and a sense of the unity of God's family, where all are of equal worth as instruments of Christ, who chooses now one, now another to do his work.

Generosity implies hospitality. No part of a Christian's life is his own exclusive property. Of course it is right for him to be part of a family or a small community, to enjoy love or friendship in privacy, all that restores him in the peace and rest he needs ; but he knows that his home and his table have to be open to welcome those who come to him. A Christian has to find a good balance between his legitimate need of peace and rest and the obligation of generous hospitality. He knows that he receives Christ when he welcomes a guest ; he puts himself at his disposal and serves him with food and with joy, and he is alert to all that he can receive from his guest.

Generosity leads to the habit of giving. A Christian is not attached to material goods or money. For him they are the means of subsistence, of allowing those entrusted to him by God to live decently, and of giving joy to those less fortunate who need his help. A Christian gives all he can, generously. He does not own anything exclusively for himself, he is a steward of the good things God has entrusted to him to share as liberally as possible with all around him.

Mercy is the charity that keeps no scores of wrong (1 Cor. 13. 5). A Christian, knowing all God has forgiven him and forgives him day after day, is always ready to forgive others their failings towards him. A Christian owes all that he has to God, and always finds it impossible to live up to the scale of God's generosity to him. A Christian is always in God's debt, and he prays : "Forgive us our debts as we forgive our debtors." He knows that God answers his prayer, showering his mercies upon him and cancelling all his debts. But he has made an undertaking in that prayer to forgive his neighbour all his little debts. A Christian forgives, as God forgives him, limitlessly.

By his spirit of forgiveness, a Christian is a sign of the mercy of God to men. Since he does not condemn or remember old scores, and turns a blind eye to failings, a Christian inspires confidence in all about him. He is a sign of the love of God, and he reassures them. A Christian can be generous with the mercy of God and distribute it lavishly around like a faithful steward who has been commissioned to administer his Master's possessions generously.

A Christian cannot harbour any resentment against his neighbour. He is always eager for reconciliation. More that that, he should go all the way to meet the other's resentment and try to dispel it, so that freely and joyously he may make his offering to God. "When you are offering your gift at the altar, and you remember your brother holds something against you, leave your gift where it is. First make it up with your brother, then come back and offer up your gift" (Matt. 5. 23-24). A Christian forgives generously and seeks forgiveness of others so that peace may reign among men. "Happy the merciful, mercy will be theirs" (Matt. 5. 7).

39

JUSTICE AND TRUTH

Christian charity takes no delight in injustice. Charity delights in the truth (1 Cor. 13. 6). The light brings a rich harvest of every kind of goodness, justice and truth (Eph. 5. 9).

Justice impels us to desire and to insist that everyone receives what we all have a right to. The Christian is a witness and an apostle of justice in the world. He cannot bear any form of inequality, oppression or tyranny. He protests, with the whole Church against the injustice which means that some starve to death while others have vast amounts of food. A Christian protests, with the whole Church, against the injustice which means that some possess too much while others have not enough to live decently. A Christian protests, with the whole Church, against the authorities of this world who are content to maintain these unjust situations to the profit of a few.

Christians pray and struggle for a just distribution of the products of the earth among all people, for cooperation in work, and for a fair share for each in the profits of every common enterprise.

Christians demand that governments should create respect, not only for law and order, but also for justice. The Church has a ministry to remind those in power of the requirements of the gospel.

In the governments of this world a Christian recognises the hidden authority of God who maintains justice and order, sustains human life and liberty, and allows the Gospel to be proclaimed. But such authority is not automatically recognised by the Church in every form of human power, whatever it may be. If a government does not defend order and justice, if it shows contempt of human life and if it absolutely denies the right to freedom of conscience and the proclamation of the gospel, the Church is free to refuse to recognise it as having legitimate authority, calling and acting for it to be replaced, in an attitude of courageous, non-violent witness ; this may result in her being persecuted. But in this case she knows that she is justified by God ; "Happy all who are persecuted for justice, the Kingdom of Heaven is theirs" (Matt. 5. 10).

The Church stands for social justice and, for his part, the individual Christian has to work for the establishment of this justice. Although the Christian may involve himself politically in the struggle for justice, the Church as a whole cannot identify her position with that of any particular party. She remains above the political choices people have to take, demanding only that whatever government is chosen, social justice, human dignity, freedom of conscience and Christian witness must be respected.

Truth, like goodness and justice, is a fruit of the light. In a Christian's regard for truth, just as in goodness and justice, people can discern a ray of the light of God. Since he believes God's word is truth, the Christian seeks to be true to himself and to others — true in what he says and what he does.

Truth in his word and his acts demands of a Christian discretion and sincerity. Since he neither desires to live in delusion nor to delude others, a

Christian has to be simple and sincere in all that he says and does. He does not lead others to believe that he feels what he does not actually feel. A Christian should be sure and trustworthy, a person others can confide in. He avoids all lying, pretence or exaggeration. Of course, he may become very enthusiastic at times. A Christian also has a sense of humour. But in everything he is candid and never deceives by a failure to be completely true in his word and his actions.

By so striving for truthfulness towards himself and others, the Christian becomes open and transparent. He makes no display of his difficulties, but his simple, sincere attitude gradually transfigures his whole being, allowing the presence of Christ in him to shine out more and more. This sincerity fills others with confidence and disposes them to receive, through the Christian who is Christ's witness, the light of the Holy Spirit. By the truthfulness of his attitude, words and actions, a Christian becomes a sign and instrument of that truth he has been called to reflect and to proclaim, the truth which is in Jesus Christ, the Light of the World.

40

CONCLUSION

Christian truth, the Christian way and the Christian life, whose basic themes we have set out, stand before us in all their beauty to the glory of God. But, at the same time as they light us with their splendour, they make plain our own unworthiness, unfitness and unfaithfulness. Here we can only ask God's forgiveness, for knowing, following and loving him so poorly. We are assured of his mercy and we ask him to lead us into the whole truth, to give us the fruit his word and the sacraments of his presence should produce in us, and to lead us in closer conformity to his will.

We ask this grace of sanctification by the truth, the way and the life of God, not for ourselves alone, but that all Christians may be led by the Holy Spirit to recover their visible unity ; that by the recovery and by the open manifestation of that unity, they may be a sign of the love of Christ for all mankind ; that all may then be led to glorify the Lord in the day of his coming, both when he calls them to faith, at the moment he chooses, and when he comes again in his glory at the end of time.

Notes

1. It is obvious that when the Epistle to the Hebrews speaks of being "sure" and "convinced", this is not the result of a rational or scientific "proof". There is proof in the eyes of faith and in terms of faith. Faith is finally an act of confidence in the truth of the Word of God; this act of confidence then discovers its own rational coherence, and interior proof of its perfect intelligibility.

2. Holy Scripture is the sure place where Christian belief finds the revelation to man of all that he needs for salvation, for sanctification and entry into eternal life. That is to say that here the Christian can be certain of finding the very Word of God, while he cannot find the same assurance of faith elsewhere. "Salvation, sanctification and eternal life": the Word of God in Holy Scripture has a purely spiritual aim. God may direct the human mind towards truths which are not of this spiritual kind; but as far as eternal salvation is concerned, the Christian knows no other place where the Word of God is explicitly expressed.

3. The "truth" in question here is obviously a theological truth, truth about God and his work of salvation, theological truth in the objective sense, as revealed to us by the Word of God contained in the Holy Scriptures.

4. The first four Councils are held to be authoritative by the greater part of Christendom. The Orthodox Churches recognize the universal normative authority of the first seven Ecumenical Councils. The Roman Catholic Church recognizes a universal normative authority in these same seven Ecumenical Councils, and in the fourteen others which she has held without the other Churches being able to join with her. It should be remembered that at the Second Vatican Council the other Churches were represented by the presence of observers — a sign of brotherly fellowship and hope for unity.

The Catholic and Orthodox Churches give a greater normative authority to tradition than do the Churches of the Reformation, which consider tradition rather as an explanation of the Word of God contained in Scripture.

The Roman Catholic Church lays great emphasis on the Magisterium of the Church, responsible for the definition and safeguard of the faith. The highest expression of the Magisterium is the infallible proclamation of a dogma by the Pope who is considered, in certain cases, to represent in his own person the faith of the Church.

5. The "whole truth" is that revealed by the Word of God, an objective, theological truth which we shall never have fully grasped with our human minds; we shall always be in a position of being able to understand better this objective truth which is the very revelation of God in Christ Jesus.

6. The Catholic and Orthodox Churches practise a veneration of the Virgin Mary, which they distinguish from the worship offered to God alone; they invoke her intercession.

The Roman Catholic Church professes the dogma of the immaculate conception of Mary, promulgated by Pope Pius IX in 1854: "The doctrine holding that the Blessed Virgin Mary was, from the first moment of her conception, preserved and kept exempt from all stain of original sin, by a special grace and particular privilege of almighty God, in view of the merits of Jesus Christ, the Saviour of mankind, is revealed by God."

The Roman Catholic Church professes the dogma of the bodily assumption of Mary, promulgated by Pope Pius XII in 1950: "It is a divinely revealed dogma that Mary, the Immaculate Mother of God, ever Virgin, was, at the end of her earthly life, raised in soul and in body to the glory of heaven."

The Orthodox Church likewise professes the doctrine of the bodily assumption of Mary, without having defined it as a dogma.

The Churches issuing from the Reformation recognize neither of these dogmas.

(*See:* Max Thurian, *Mary, Mother of the Lord, Figure of the Church*, Faith Press, England.)

7. Roman Catholic theology considers that the eternal salvation of each individual is decided in this life. *See* notes 12 and 13.

8. The Roman Catholic Church considers that, in spite of the divisions between Christians, she has preserved the visible unity desired by Christ, guaranteed by the union of bishops with the Pope.

   The Orthodox Church considers that, in spite of the divisions between Christians, she has preserved the fullness of the truth in her tradition and liturgy, and that this fullness of truth is necessary for visible untiy.

   The Churches issuing from the Reformation consider that, in spite of the divisions between Christians, the essential unity has been maintained; but this essential unity of the Body of Christ is not enough, it must be manifested in the visible union of the Churches, in the unity of the truth, in mutual recognition of ministries and in communion at the same Holy Table.

9. The Roman Catholic Church considers that the indefectibility of the Church implies the infallibility of the Pope, a dogma promulgated by Pope Pius IX in 1870 with the approval of the First Vatican Council: "Whenever the Roman Pontiff speaks *ex cathedra*, i.e. when, in fulfilment of his office as pastor and teacher of all Christians, he defines in virtue of his supreme apostolic authority that a doctrine on faith or on morals shall be held by the whole Church, he enjoys by the divine assistance promised to him in the person of St Peter that infallibility which the Divine Redeemer willed his Church to possess when she defines doctrine on faith or on morals. Consequently, such definitions by the Roman Pontiff are irrevocable in themselves, and not by virtue of the assent of the Church."

10. Those Churches which possess sacramental episcopacy, conceived as the fullness of the ministry, (Catholic, Orthodox, Anglican . . .), consider that the apostolicity of the ministry is assured in the apostolic succession, transmitted by the consecration of bishops by bishops, in a transmission unbroken since the Church began.

The Churches issuing from the Reformation which have kept the historic episcopate see in it an ecumenical ministry and a sign of unity, not an absolute necessity for ensuring the apostolic succession, the continuity and validity of the ministry. *See* note 21.

11. The Catholic and Orthodox Churches practise a veneration of the saints, which they distinguish from the worship offered to God alone; they invoke their intercession.

    The Anglican Church and some of the Lutheran Churches make memory in their liturgy of the saints, their lives, their witness and their prayers; they set them forth as an example for Christians.

12. Catholic theology, which considers that the eternal salvation of every human being is decided in this life, has never really developed this notion of the "dwelling of the dead".

13. The Roman Catholic Church teaches that hell is the state of suffering in which all who die rejecting God (in "mortal sin") stay for ever — although, created as they are in the image of God, they can never be satisfied except by him.

    The Churches issuing from the Reformation have the same teaching in their tradition, believing it to be contained in Holy Scripture.

    Today we find it hard to reconcile belief in the infinite mercy of the Father with these eternal torments of hell reserved for those who have denied Christ. On the other hand, revelation affirms the judgment of God upon those guilty of the sin against the Holy Spirit. For some, the biblical theme of the second death, understood as the final annihilation of the "damned" — instead of eternal suffering — permit both the affirmation of the justice of God and trust in his infinite mercy.

    The Roman Catholic Church teaches the doctrine of Purgatory; this is the state of sorrowful waiting for peace in which the righteous dead remain, so long as their charity is contradicted by sinful events in their lives which have been forgiven but not atoned for. Therefore the Catholic Church practices prayer for the faithful departed, so that they may be delivered from their waiting in purgatory.

The Orthodox Church does not teach the doctrine of purgatory, but also practises prayer for the departed.

The Churches issuing from the Reformation do not profess the doctrine of purgatory, nor admit it.

14. Baptism unites all Christians, in spite of their divisions; it unites them to the Body of Christ and thus sets them in profound communion with one another. In general, all Churches recognize the baptism of every Christian; this makes Baptism the supreme sacrament of ecumenical unity.

15. The Churches issuing from the Reformation emphasize particularly the fact that the Eucharist is a gift of the real presence of Christ and all the graces which accompany that presence, for our sanctification.

   The Catholic Church emphasizes the gift of the real presence of Christ, but equally emphasizes the sacrificial and propitiatory character of the mass, which obtains from God remission of sins for the living and the dead.

   The Churches issuing from the Reformation teach the real presence of Christ, his body and his blood, in the Eucharist, but they do not specify the mode of this presence.

   The Catholic Church teaches that by the consecration of the bread and wine a change is effected, by which the total substance of the bread is changed into the substance of the body of Christ and the total substance of the wine is changed into the substance of his blood. She declares that this change is rightly and accurately called "transsubstantiation" (Council of Trent, 13th Session 1551, chap. 4). The Catholic Church reserves the consecrated hosts (wafers) for communion to be given outside the mass (especially to the sick and dying), and also for the adoration of the sacrament.

16. The Catholic Church considers confirmation as one of the seven sacraments; it is celebrated, with certain exceptions, by the bishop.

17. The Catholic Church considers confession as one of the seven sacraments. Primitive Lutheran tradition also recognised the sacramental character of absolution.

18. The Catholic Church specified its concept of the sacrament of the sick at the Second Vatican Council: "Extreme unction, which is also more properly called the anointing of the sick, is not only the sacrament for those in imminent danger of death. The moment has come to receive it when death begins to be a possibility because of physical weakness or old age" (Constitution: *Sacrosanctum Concilium*, article 73).

19. The Catholic Church considers marriage as one of the seven sacraments. She does not admit divorce and re-marriage of divorced persons, except in certain cases which must be submitted to the authority of Rome. This position is very consistent with the teaching of Christ, although it sometimes creates difficult situations for the Christian life of divorced persons who have remarried. But the more flexible attitude of the Reformation Churches also gives rise to difficult situations. It would be desirable for the Churches to arrive at a common, ecumenical ruling on this issue.

20. *See:* Brother Roger, Prior of Taizé, *Living Today for God* (Mowbray).

21. Those Churches which have sacramental episcopacy, conceived as the fullness of the ministry, (Catholic, Orthodox, Anglican . . .), consider that only a bishop can ordain, although the bishop is surrounded by priests at ordinations.

    The Churches issuing from the Reformation believe in ordination by the college of presbyters or pastors, which may be presided over by a bishop.

22. The Catholic Church considers that the bishop is not only a presbyter (priest or pastor) who receives new ecumenical responsibility, the ministry to be the pastor of pastors, authority over a larger area of the Church and a service of unity, but is also endowed with the fullness of priesthood from which that of priests derives.